Simple BASIC 2 Programs on the Amstrad PC 1512 1640

Second Edition

Robin Kinge, Marc Diprose & P.K. McBride

Heinemann   London

Heinemann Professional Publishing Ltd
22 Bedford Square, London WC1B 3HH

LONDON   MELBOURNE   JOHANNESBURG   AUCKLAND

First published by Newtech Books Ltd 1986
First published by Heinemann Professional Publishing Ltd 1987

ISBN 0 434 91078 3

Designed by John Clark and Associates, Ringwood, Hampshire

Printed in the UK by HGA Printing Co. Ltd, Brentford, Middlesex

Contents

Contents

PART THREE   SUMMARY OF BASIC2 KEYWORDS

PART ONE

Introduction

■ SECTION 1
Getting started

There have been many variations of the Basic programming language since it was first developed just over twenty years ago, but so far there has been nothing that can match Basic 2 in terms of speed or versatility.

Basic has always been an ideal language for beginners. It is easy to understand, and friendly to use. The ability to test out single commands or short routines, without having to write a full program, is a great help, as is the way that the language checks for errors and lets you know where and why you have gone wrong. The better versions of Basic give you simple access to all of the functions of the computer — its graphics, number-crunching, text-handling, disk storage and the rest. Basic is also a good beginner's language because it is very tolerant of poor programming habits, so that those of us who are not very disciplined in our approach, can still produce something that does what we want it to do. (Though the more organised you are, the more successful you will be).

Basic 2 is as user-friendly as most versions of the language — though it could be a little more helpful over errors; what counts for more in the long run is that it has a superb command set, giving excellent control of all aspects of your PC — the graphics and the disk-management commands are remarkably comprehensive. Of course, it does mean that there are well over 200 words in the language — twice as many as in some dialects — but you do not have to learn them all at once, and you will be glad that they are all there in the end.

This very comprehensive command set, and the sheer speed at which Basic 2 programs run, mean that the language can be used for professional applications. Other, earlier, versions of the language have just been too slow for serious programming, as anyone who has tried to use a Basic business program will testify. This isn't the case with Basic 2. Now you have a user-friendly language that can produce fast, efficient, and very attractive programs for business - and for pleasure.

8

■ SECTION 1
Getting started

If you are a complete beginner then you shouldn't find it too hard to get started with Basic 2, and the stunning screen effects that can be produced by very simple programs are a great stimulus to further effort. If you have already done some programming with other dialects of Basic, then your skills will transfer readily — once you have got over your surprise at finding that there are *no line numbers*! Don't worry, you'll soon realise that you don't need them.

Step by Step Basic is designed around the belief that the best way to learn programming is by doing it. The key concepts and commands are introduced and demonstrated first. This is then followed by a series of annotated programs that will illustrate different aspects of programming, and show many of the other commands in operation. Please experiment with these to try the effects of using commands in different ways, and please feel free to develop your own programs that build on the ones given here. At the end is a summary of the Basic 2 commands. This is for reference when you are working through our programs, and when you are writing your own.

Getting started

Basic 2 works within the GEM Desktop, and is supplied on Disk 3 which also contains the Desktop utilities. It makes sense, therefore, to use a COPY (never use the master disks!) of that disk as your desktop disk.

1 Have the GEM Desktop running, with the Basic2 disk in drive A (the one on the left if you have two floppy drives) and display the root directory (A:\) in a window, If you have a hard disk, the root directory is C:\.If you are currently working on another folder, you may need to click the Close icon (the 'bow-tie' at the extreme left of the top line) until you get back to the Root directory.

2 Look for the Basic2 folder amongst the icons.

3 Move the pointer to the Basic2 folder and double-click the left-hand mouse button. You should see the display shown below. If you don't get it, try this:

Click the Basic2 folder once so that it is highlighted; point to the **File** label on the top line to pull its menu down, point to and click the **Open** option.

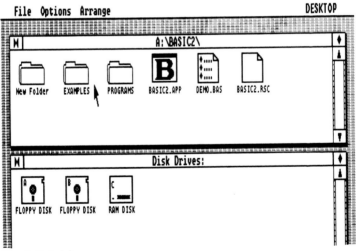

Basic2 folders

Either method can be used to gain access to a folder or a file.

4 Move the pointer to the Basic 2 icon (the big B) and double-click to select it. Basic 2 will then be read into memory and the screen will change to give the Basic window display.

■ SECTION 2
Finding your way round the screen

The standard Basic screen has five parts to it; four windows and a string along the top.

File Program Edit Fonts Colours Patterns Lines Windows   BASIC2

Basic screen

A **Window** is not simply a box marked out on the main screen. It is a frame through which you can view part of another, independent screen. Windows are not fixed. They can be moved or removed, or changed in size and shape, either with the mouse or by Basic 2 commands. A window can sit on top of another, obscuring it, but revealing it again as soon as it is moved. The screen that you can see through a window is stored in memory almost as if it were a full-size screen, though in fact only part is visible. You can change your view by scrolling this screen up and down, left and right, without moving the window. As a new part of the screen is exposed, the GEM system will quickly draw or write on any material that is supposed to be there.

The top left window, labelled **Dialogue** is used for talking directly to Basic 2. It is here that you will type those commands that are to be acted upon immediately, and those that affect the program as a whole - such as **RUN, STOP, CONT** and **EDIT**. When you type **EDIT**, you will be moved into the lower left window.

The **Edit** window is where you will write and edit your Basic 2 programs. The commands that are typed in here will be stored in sequence and not acted upon until you return to the Dialogue window and type **RUN**.

The large window on the right is labelled **Results-1**. It is here that the effects of commands, whether given directly, or in a program, will be displayed.

There is a further window **Results-2** that is normally hidden underneath the Dialogue and Edit windows. It will appear briefly as the screen is being organised, and can be revealed by moving the other windows out of the way. *Results-2 may not always be present.* If some memory is already tied up, from previous operations, when you load Basic 2, then there may not be sufficient for it to manage all four windows. If you need the second Results window, and it isn't there, then reset the PC and start it up again from scratch.

Either of the Results windows can be used for text only, or for text and graphics. Results-1 may therefore be all you actually need. However, as text screens offer a quicker and more convenient method of handling text, there are advantages to keeping text and graphics separate, and in this case, you will need both of the windows.

The top strip of the Basic display shows the names of Menus:

File Program Edit Fonts Colours Patterns Lines Windows BASIC2

If you point to one of these with the mouse, the menu that unrolls will display the options available to you under that heading. We will take these one at a time later as we need them.

If you have not already done so, now would be a good time to look at the DEMO.BAS program that is supplied on the Basic 2 disk. Use the mouse to point at **File** and click to pull down the menu. Point to **Load** and click it. The Item Selector box will appear on screen, showing the files on the disk. Select DEMO.BAS. Type **RUN** in the Dialogue window and press Return. You will be treated to a sequence of short routines that will demonstrate some of the capabilities of Basic2. The program will list, in the Edit window, those commands that are creating the effects in the Results-1 window.

Instant results

Time for you to do something! For the moment we will stay in the Dialogue window, as we are going to give commands that are to be acted upon immediately.

Type in something like this:

print "A small step for a mouse, but a giant step for computerkind."

The message you use is up to you, but you must use the command **print** and enclose the text in quotes. Press the Return key - the long one with the left arrow - when you have finished, and the command will be passed to Basic 2 for processing. Immediately afterwards, your text will appear on the Results-1 screen.

Try PRINTing a few more messages - remembering the quotes and Return at the end. If you mistype the command or forget the first set of quotes (it doesn't matter if you omit the closing set), then Basic 2 will type **Syntax error** in the Dialogue window. Spot the mistake, and try again.

```
   File  Program  Edit  █Fonts█  Colours  Patterns  Lines  Windows      BASIC2
┌─┬───────────────────┬──────────────────────────┬────────────────────────
│H│     Dialogue      │ ▸ 1 System               │        Results-1
├─┴───────────────────┤   2 Swiss                │
│Locomotive BASIC 2   │   3 Dutch                │
│(c) Copyright 1986   │   4 Loadable             │
│Locomotive Software Ltd│━━━━━━━━━━━━━━━━━━━━━━━━│
│All rights reserved  │     7 Point    18 Point  │
│                     │   8 Point    20 Point    │
│Ready                │ ▸ 10 Point    24 Point   │
│█                    │   12 Point    28 Point   │
│                     │   14 Point  ▶ 36 Point   │
│                     │   16 Point  ╲72 Point    │
│                     │━━━━━━━━━━━━━━━━━━━━━━━━│
├─────────────────────┤   Thickened              │
│.....................│   Lightened              │
│.....................│   Skewed                 │
│        Edit         │   Underlined             │
└─────────────────────┴──────────────────────────┘
```

Fonts menu

■ SECTION 3
Instant results

You can vary the appearance of your text using the **Fonts** menu. Use the mouse to point to **Fonts** and pull the menu down. It is divided into three sections. At the top you will see the choice of fonts, or typefaces. There should be a small arrow next to **System**, at the top. This is the *default* font - the one selected by Basic 2 at startup. You can change it to **Swiss** or **Dutch** by pointing to the name and clicking the mouse button. Print some text in your new typeface to see what it looks like.

The size and style of the text can also be varied by the Fonts menu. Pull it down again, and turn your attention to the middle section. **Point** refers to type-size. The default value is 10 Point. Click on a larger number for bigger characters. Pull the menu down again to alter the style. Click on each one in turn, and print another message to see the effects. Not all of the point sizes are available for every Font. The ones that can be used are shown in highlighted characters.

The third section of the Fonts menu changes the style of the text, to give such effects as bold and italic text.

Note that these effects can be combined. You can have **Thickened, Skewed, Underlined** text - if you really want to emphasise something. To turn off a style, point to it and click again.

There's one last menu to look at before we leave printing for a while. Pull down the **Colours** menu and click on a new colour in the top - TEXT section of the menu.

It should soon become very obvious that Basic 2, and the Amstrad PC, will allow you to produce some very interesting textual effects, that can add a lot of impact to your screen displays.

When you have finished exploring the different fonts, or when the Results screen is geting too cluttered, type:

    cls

CLS means Clear Screen, and will wipe away all your text.

■ SECTION 3
Instant results

Let's have a quick look at some of those graphics commands that you will have seen in use in the demonstration program. Type:

circle 2500;2500,500 [and Return]

You should now see a large circle in the centre of the Results screen. When Basic 2 is handling graphics, it treats the screen as if it was a sheet of graph paper, with co-ordinates running from 0 to 5000, from left to right, and from bottom to top. The numbers that followed that CIRCLE command told Basic to draw a circle with the centre 2500 points from the left and from the bottom, and 500 points in radius. Add another, smaller, circle to the screen:

circle 1000;4000,250

This will appear towards the top left of the screen, as the x co-ordinate - the one that fixes the horizontal position has been reduced to 1000, while the y co-ordinate - the vertical - has been increased to 4000.

Let's bring a little colour into this. Point to the **Colours** label and pull down that menu. You will notice a little arrow next to the colour being used at the moment. Point to another colour in the GRAPHICS half of the menu, and click it. Repeat one of those circle commands, and it will be drawn in the new colour.

The line style can also be altered very simply and in much the same way. Point to **Lines** and pull down the menu. There are three parts to this. The top section shows the type of line - continuous, dotted, broken, etc.; the middle section gives a choice of thicknesses (for continuous lines only); and the bottom part shows the choice of ends. As we are drawing circles, the ends are irrelevant at the moment. Use the mouse to click a new choice of styles and thickness. You will notice that the menu disappears as soon as a selection is made, and so must be pulled down again for a second selection - which can be annoying if you want to fix the end-of-line type for both ends!

16

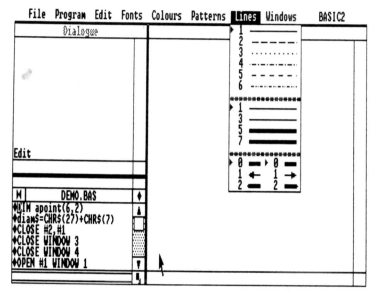

Lines menu

Try some more circles, using different colours and lines, and varying the figures so that you get the feel of the co-ordinate system. If you get an error message, then check the punctuation in the command. There should be a space after the command, a semi-colon (;) between the x and y figures, and a comma before the radius. Don't worry about the circles going off the screen. Basic 2 can handle that. When the screen starts to get cluttered, use CLS to clear it.

Here's a second graphics command that gives impressive results for very little effort. It is **BOX** and it draws a rectangle. To use it, you must give the x,y co-ordinates of the bottom left hand corner, and its width and height - in that order:

box 2000;1000,500,1500

This will give you an outline of an upright bar 500 points wide and 1500 high, and it will be drawn in the current line-type and colour. These can be varied using the **Lines** and **Colours** menus, just as they can for circles, and any other graphics.

17

Instant results

If you want a solid, filled box, you only have to say so:

box 3000;2000,1000,500 fill

Watch the punctuation! Semi-colon between the x and y co-ordinates, as before, and commas between the other numbers. Space, but no punctuation, before the **fill**.

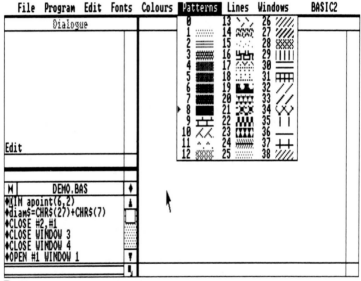

Patterns menu

The box should be filled with the current colour. This infill does not have to be solid. You can vary it with the **Patterns** menu. Use the mouse to pull it down onto the screen. With a choice of 39 patterns to hand, you will realise the colourful, attractive displays are easy to achieve. Explore some of them with different sizes and shapes of box. You can also produce filled circles in exactly the same way.

circle 1000;1500,750 fill

CIRCLE and BOX are only two of many graphics commands, and we will return to these later in Section 11, but now it's time to take a more significant step - from direct commands to programs.

■ SECTION 4
Starting programming

In your experimentations with CIRCLE and BOX you may have come across particular sequences of commands that produced displays that you might like to repeat in the future. If you do this with direct commands - through the Dialogue window - then you will have to type them in afresh every time. By linking them into a program, and saving it on disk, you can repeat them any time you like, without having to re-type.

The simplest types of programs are those that perform a fixed sequence of commands. In practice, you will rarely come across a full program that follows a single straight line, but you will find simple sequences within programs - in particular, for producing graphic or text displays. Let's try one.

First, you need to gain access to the **Edit** window. There are three ways of doing this. Either type **Edit** in the Dialogue window, or pull down the **Program** menu and click on **Edit**, or press **f10**.

I find the default size Edit window a bit too small for serious use, so I like to stretch it before starting work. You might like to do this too.

Use the mouse to point to any place within the top (title) bar. Hold down the left-hand mouse button, and drag the window up the screen until the Dialogue window is half covered. (You should see a thin outline moving. If you don't, go back to the title line and try to pick it up again). Release the button, and move the mouse to point to the small box at the extreme bottom right of the window. Hold the left-hand button down and as you move the mouse, the window should change size. Drag it down to the bottom of the screen - you might also like to widen it a little, but don't obscure too much of the Results-1 window.

We will look again at windows and screen displays in Section 108.

Remove the DEMO.BAS program by pulling down the **Program** menu and clicking on **New**.

Type in your own sequence of graphics commands, or use the example given below.

First, a few points about keying-in programs:

■ SECTION 4
Starting programming

1 **Always type in** *lower case* **characters.** Basic 2 will check each line as you finish it, and convert all command words into *UPPER CASE*. If a word is not converted, it shows that you have mistyped it. In the examples given in this book, the keywords are printed in CAPITALS, to show how the lines should appear after they have been checked.

2 **Press the Return key at the end of each command line.** A complex line, written in a narrow window, may take up more than one line on screen. Only press Return at the end of the *logical* (command) line. To check the lines, look for a black diamond at the beginning of each command line. Overflow lines start with a hyphen.

3 **To edit a line,** move the cursor (the black rectangle) up to the error using the mouse or the cursor keys. Note that the cursor keys may be switched off at first. To bring them into use press CTRL (ConTRoL).

To remove a character, position the cursor on the next character along and press the DELete Left key.

To remove a whole line, delete back from the right hand end.

To insert a character, position the cursor to the right of where it needs to go, and type. The rest of the line will shuffle up to make room.

To insert a new line, place the cursor at the start of the next line and press Return. Move the cursor back up to the new line space, and type.

4 You do not have to type in the whole program in one session. You can stop at any time and test the commands written up to that point, by *running* the program. You can do this in three ways;
either use the mouse to pull down the **Program** menu, and select **Run**;
or press **f9**. (Both methods will make the word **Run** appear in the Dialogue window, as if it had been typed there).
The third method is to leave the Edit window, by pulling

Starting programming

down the **Program** menu and clicking **Exit Edit**. Then you can type Run in the Dialogue window.

However you do it, RUN will make the PC run through the program's commands. When it reaches the end, you can get back into the Edit window and make any additions or alterations that you need.

5   **When you do run the program**, Basic 2 will check each line as it comes to it. If it meets an instruction that it cannot obey, it will stop and print an error message in the Dialogue window. At the same time, you will see that the cursor has been moved to the beginning of a line in the Edit window. This is the line that has the error. While you are working through the examples in the first part of this book, it should be simple enough to find an error by comparing your lines with those given. Later, when you are tackling more complex projects, you will need to know more about how to find - and cure - errors. We will return to this in Section 20.

```
REM Locomotive Graphics?
REM This uses circle and box commands
REM REMarks don't actually do anything
REM They are there to explain things
WINDOW #1, FULL ON
BOX 2000;1000,1750,750
BOX 3500;1750,250,750
BOX 2500;1750,250,750
BOX 2000;2400,500,100
CIRCLE 2200;800,200
CIRCLE 2650;800,200
CIRCLE 3100;800,200
CIRCLE 3500;800,200
CIRCLE 3250;3000,200
CIRCLE 2800;3100,300
CIRCLE 2500;3250,400
LABEL wait
GOTO wait
```

Click on the Results-1 window before you run the program. To stop the program pull down the **Program** menu and click on **Stop**.

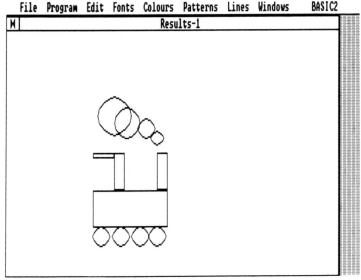

File Program Edit Fonts Colours Patterns Lines Windows   BASIC2

Results-1

Locomotive graphics?

If you have used the Locomotive Graphics example, then you might like to go back to the program after you have Run it, and make a few alterations. Adding FILL to the end of the BOX and some of the CIRCLE commands might improve the appearance. Don't forget that you can also alter the display by selecting Colours, Line styles and Patterns from the menus before you start. It is also possible, and simple, to change these things within Basic command lines. We will return to this at Section 11.

If you want to retain any of your trial programs for later use, then they can be saved on a disk. To do this, first make sure that you have a disk in the drive, then point to and pull down the **Files** menu. Click on **Save**. The Item Selector box will appear. Notice the vertical bar cursor at the start of the Selection line. Type in a suitable name - without using spaces. (Put an underline character in if you want to leave a gap.) **Do not attempt to store them on a Master Disk!**

■ SECTION 5
Storing data

Graphics are fun, and a good way to start programming because you can get impressive results with a few simple commands. They also have serious applications, for example in Computer Aided Design, and the display of business statistics; and are an important part of the presentation of many types of programs. However, graphics alone will not get you very far. The main uses of computers are for storing and processing data.

A computer's memory is organised into bytes, each consisting of eight bits - Binary digITs - which can be set to '0' or '1'. (Electronically, this is the presence or absence of an electric current, or the direction of a magnetic field). Because of the nature of binary arithmetic (which we needn't go into at this stage) a single byte can hold any number up to 255. These can be actual values, or the code numbers that represent different characters.

Every byte in the memory has its own unique *address*, and if you are working in machine code, it is your responsibility as a programmer to keep track of the addresses you use. This is hard work, calling for a great deal of care and discipline. Fortunately, Basic provides a simpler way to store data. It uses *variables*.

A variable is a named area of memory. Where it is, is irrelevant to you as a programmer. All you have to do is remember the name under which you stored an item of data. These names can be meaningful, and as short or as long as you like up to a maximum of 40 characters. There are a few simple rules you must follow:

1   Variables can be written in either upper or lower case, but are treated as the same. 'AGE' and 'age' all refer to the same variable.

2   You may use any characters except spaces and arithmetical symbols, and % : # and $ may only be used at the end of names. $ has a special meaning - see 4 below.

3   You must not use any of the Basic command words.

■ SECTION 5
Storing data

4 Basic 2 recognises two types of data - numbers and text. These are held in numeric and string variables. String variables - so-called because they hold *strings* of characters - are distinguished by a **$** at the end of the name; eg. title$, first_name$, surname$. They are effectively of unlimited size. (How long is a piece of string?)

A string can be anything between 1 and 4096 characters long. Numbers can be stored in string variables, but only as a string of digits. For normal use, their values are stored in numeric variables. These must not end in **$**.

Data that has been stored in a variable is freely available within a program, for whatever kind of processing you need; it can be used within calculations, or copied to the screen, printer, onto disk or to another part of memory. Unless you deliberately over-write it, the data will not be altered or lost until you run the program, load in a new one, use the **Clear** command or leave Basic 2.

INPUT

There are several ways of getting data into variables. The first method we will look at is from the keyboard, using the command **INPUT**. Try this program to see how it works:

```
REM  Details, Please
WINDOW #1, FULL ON
CLS #1
PRINT "I would like a few details . . ."
PRINT "Let's start with your surname."
INPUT surname$
INPUT "First name";first$
INPUT "Age";age
PRINT first$;" "surname$;" is ";age;" years old."
STOP
REM STOP signals the end of the program
REM It is not actually necessary in this case
```

Run the program when you have finished typing, and answer when it prompts you for your details. (Don't forget that you can alter the Fonts or the Colours by selecting from the menus. This can be done *while the program is running,* as well as before it starts).

■ SECTION 5
Storing data

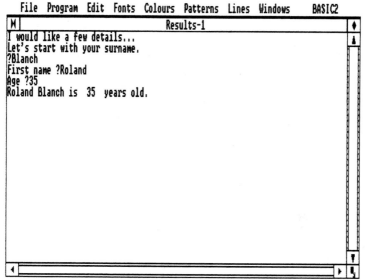

File	Program	Edit	Fonts	Colours	Patterns	Lines	Windows		BASIC2

```
M                          Results-1
I would like a few details...
Let's start with your surname.
?Blanch
First name ?Roland
Age ?35
Roland Blanch is  35  years old.
```

Personal details please

A few points to notice about the PRINT and INPUT commands.

At the simplest, PRINT will type on the screen the text that is given in quotes. It can also type out the contents of any variables, and there can be more than one item in a PRINT line. In this event, you will need some punctuation between them. Use a semi-colon where you want the items to appear next to each other; or a comma to create a larger space.

INPUT must be followed by a variable name - **INPUT surname$**, but the line can also include a prompt - **INPUT "AGE";age**. This saves having to write a separate PRINT line for the prompt. You can only use text (in quotes) in the prompt, and the punctuation after it follows the normal PRINT rules.

Storing data

It is also possible to include several different variables in one INPUT command:

INPUT "x,y co-ordinates?";x,y

When this line is performed, the user will have to either type a comma, or press Return , between the two figures that are given. Some programmers like to use this kind of multiple input to save typing, but separate input lines are generally less confusing, and therefore more satisfactory from the user's point of view.

LET

A second method of getting data into a variable is to use the **LET** command. This assigns a given value, from within the program. eg.

LET first_number = 6
LET second_number = 7
LET result = first_number * second_number
LET message$ = "The answer is"
PRINT message$;result
STOP

Notice that the variable to which you are assigning a value is always written on the left of the equals sign. This is the opposite way round to normal arithmetic, where the answer is usually on the right. You should also notice that the value that you assign can be given directly:

LET first_number = 6

or can be taken from another variable, or be the result of a calculation:

LET result = first_number + second_number

It is worth adding that **LET** is not necessary.

first_number = 6

will work just as well, but the use of the word does help to make the program easier to understand.

There are other ways to assign values to variables, and we will return to them in Section 114. It's time now to take a further step with the structure of our programs.

Could you repeat that?

A computer's ability to repeat sequences of actions - perhaps for many thousands of times, and without ever getting bored - is one of its greatest assets. It is also an essential part of most data-processing, enabling a few lines to do a lot of work.

Basic 2 gives you four alternative ways to loop around a sequence of commands.

The FOR .... NEXT loop

This is used where you want to perform something a set number of times, or to process a particular series of numbers, e.g.

```
PRINT "The Times Table Program"
INPUT "Times what?";multiplier
FOR count = 1 TO 10
result = count + multiplier
PRINT count;"times ";multiplier;" equals ";result
NEXT count
```

The variable **count** starts with a value of 1. When the program works through to the **NEXT** line, its value is increased by 1, and checked against the value given after **TO** ... Here it is 10. As long as the value of **count** is less than or equal to 10, the program will go back to the first line within the loop (**result** = .. .). When the value of the loop variable goes beyond the limit, the computer will move onto the next part of the program, if any.

The name used for the loop variable can be any valid variable name. You do not have to write it after the **NEXT** command, as Basic 2 will work out which one to use.

You do not have to work through a set of numbers one at a time. The size and type of step that you take can be written into the **FOR** .. line.

```
FOR lines = 1 TO 20 STEP 4
PRINT AT (1,lines);"Line number ";lines
NEXT lines
```

This will print a message on lines number 1, 5, 9, 13 and 17. After the next STEP, **lines** would have a value of 21, which overruns the loop limit. The **PRINT AT** command makes the text start at a given column and line number, with the top left corner being 1,1.

Try changing the value of the **first, last** and **stepsize** variables in this program, and see the different effects. **last** can be smaller than **first**. If it is, then **stepsize** must be a negative number,

```
CLS
INPUT "Start at..";first
INPUT "Finish at..";last
INPUT "In steps of..";stepsize
FOR radius = first TO last STEP stepsize
CIRCLE 2500;2500,250 * radius
NEXT radius
```

REPEAT ... UNTIL

In this type of loop, an action or set of actions is repeated until a particular condition is met.

```
x = 0
REPEAT
PRINT x
x = x + 1
UNTIL x = 100
```

It is useful for checking inputs. In the earlier 'Personal Details' program, we could have included a request for the user's sex, and made sure that we got an 'M' or 'F' reply in this way:

```
REPEAT
INPUT "Sex (M/F) ";sex$
UNTIL sex$ = "M" OR sex$ = "F"
```

WHILE ..... WEND

A REPEAT ... UNTIL loop will always go through its commands at least once. Sometimes you will not want this. If you only want to go into a loop on certain conditions, then WHILE ..... WEND is the structure to use. This checks on the loop condition before it performs the commands.

```
INPUT "Give me a number below 100 ";num
WHILE num >= 100
PRINT "That is too large."
INPUT "Below 100, please ";num
WEND
PRINT "Thank you."
```

The WHILE line checks to see if the value of **num** is greater than or equal to 100. If it is, then the program will perform the loop, otherwise it will jump right over to the "Thank you" line.

GOTO

Although GOTO provides a very simple method of creating loops, it has been left until last because it raises a couple of complications.

In earlier, standard, versions of Basic, the command GOTO is followed by the number of the line to which the program must jump. For instance:

```
100 PRINT "Help! I am a prisoner in an endless loop!"
110 GOTO 100
```

In Basic 2 there are no line numbers. Instead, you mark points to which you want to jump by using **LABEL**s. The rules for label names are the same as for variable names.

```
LABEL loopstart
PRINT "Help! I am still locked in a loop!"
GOTO loopstart
```

You can jump to any LABELled line from anywhere else in a program, but if you jump back in a loop - as happens here - you have a problem, as should be obvious. How do you get out?

There are two methods of escaping from a GOTO loop. The first is to press **CTRL** and **C**. This breaks into the program and forces it to stop. Further on in the book you will find several graphic display programs that end with closed GOTO loops. If they weren't there, then as soon as the graphics commands had been executed, the program would end and the Edit and Dialogue windows would reappear on the screen, spoiling the display. The GOTO loop keeps the program running - albeit in circles - until you force it to stop.

The second way of getting out of a GOTO loop is to write an escape line into the loop. And that takes us to the next step.

■ SECTION 7
Branching out

IF .... THEN

This structure allows you to test the value in a variable. **IF** it meets the given conditions **THEN** the computer will perform the next command. If it doesn't, the program moves on to the next line. Let's use it to escape from a GOTO loop. Here, you must give the correct password to get into the program.

```
LABEL doorkeeper
INPUT "Password Please ";pass$
IF pass$ = "Open Sesame" THEN GOTO begin.program
GOTO doorkeeper
LABEL begin.program
....
```

If you think about the way that loops were used in the last Section you will realise that this same operation could be done more simply with a REPEAT .... UNTIL loop.

```
REPEAT
INPUT "Password Please ";pass$
UNTIL pass$ = "Open Sesame"
```

Using IF .... THEN to jump out of a loop makes more sense where you have a number of possible exits. Suppose that you have displayed a menu of options and are reading the keyboard, waiting for one of several keys to be pressed. The routine might look like this:

```
PRINT "Load a file (L), Save a file (S) or End (E)?"
PRINT "Please press a key"
LABEL keyloop
ky$ = INKEY$
IF ky$ = "L" THEN GOTO load.file
IF ky$ = "S" THEN GOTO save.file
IF ky$ = "E" THEN STOP
GOTO keyloop
....
....
LABEL load.file
....
```

....
LABEL save_file
....
....

Three points to note about this example.

1 The command after THEN does not have to be a GOTO jump. It can be any command. Where it is a GOTO, you can miss out THEN.

IF ky$ = "L" GOTO load_file

This will work just as well.

2 A new command has been used - **INKEY$**. This reads the keyboard, one character at a time, without printing it on the screen, and without waiting for the Return key to be pressed. The character can be passed to a variable for checking. It is a much simpler way to get a single key response than using INPUT, and as the character is not printed on the screen, the display is not affected.

3 This only checks for capital letters. Press the right key, without SHIFT, and it will be ignored. There are a couple of simple ways to make either form of a letter acceptable:

IF UPPER$(ky$) = "L" THEN ....

This ensures that the character in ky$ is in upper case. The similar command **LOWER$** forces characters into lower case. Either can be applied to long strings as well as to single characters.

IF ky$ = "L" OR ky$ = "l" THEN ...

When **OR** is used, the command after THEN will be performed if either of the conditions is met, or if they both are.

■ SECTION 7
Branching out

CONDITION TESTING

All **IF .... THEN** lines depend upon condition testing. The program will check the value of one or more variables, and only perform the command after THEN if the conditions are satisfied. These checks operate in much the same way whether they are on numbers or strings. A variable can be compared with a value in any of six ways:

$<$ **less than**
$>$ **greater than**
$=$ **equal to**
$<=$ **less than or equal to**
$>=$ **greater than or equal to**
$<>$ **not equal to**

Where numbers are concerned, the way these tests work is obvious. With strings there is a little more to it.

Characters are compared on the basis of their ASCII codes. ASCII is short for American Standard Codes for Information Interchange, and the codes for letters, digits and punctuation (those between 32 and 127) are the same on all computers. Thus 32 is the code for space, 65 refers to 'A', 66 to 'B', 97 to 'a', and so on.

When a string variable is compared with another, or with a given character or string, it is the code numbers that are being compared. So, 'A' is less than 'B', but 'a' (ASCII 97) is greater than 'Z' (ASCII 90).

If there are several characters in the strings, then each letter in turn is compared until a difference is found. If the characters are *digits* it can lead to some apparently odd results. All of the following comparisons give a true answer:

> "eel" $<$ "elephant"
> "anteater" $>$ "aardvark"
> "a" $>$ "Z"
> "123" $<=$ "12345"
> "2" $>$ "10" (though **2** $<$ **10** as numbers)

■ SECTION 7
Branching out

If you need to check more than one condition, you can do it either through a series of tests and branches or by using the *logical operators* – **AND, OR, XOR** and **NOT**.

AND is used where two, or more, conditions must be true.

> **IF answer > 0 AND answer < 99 THEN GOTO carry.on**

This line is the same as:

> **IF answer > 0 THEN GOTO test.top**
>
> ....
> **LABEL test.top**
> **IF answer < 99 THEN GOTO carry.on**

OR is used where the commands are to be performed if any one or all of the conditions in the line are true:

> **IF ky$ = "L" OR ky$ = "I" THEN ...**

XOR is used where it is essential that only if one, but not both, of the conditions is true:

> **IF num.1 > 100 XOR num.2 > 100 THEN ....**

NOT is used to reverse the truth of a statement, so that

> **IF NOT a = 99 THEN ....**

is the same as:

> **IF a <> 99 THEN ....**

We can pull some of these ideas together in a routine that will find the appropriate title for a person, based on data about their age, sex and marital status:

```
REM Mr. and Mrs.
INPUT "Your age, please ";age
INPUT "Your sex, please (M/F) ";sex$
INPUT "Married or Single (M/S) ";status$
IF sex$ = "F" THEN GOTO female
title$ = "Mr."
IF age < 18 THEN title$ = "Master"
GOTO print_out
LABEL female
title$ = "Mrs."
IF age < 18 AND status = "S" THEN title$ = "Miss"
IF age > 18 AND status <> "M" THEN title$ = "Ms"
LABEL print_out
....
```

■ SECTION 8
Number crunching

Basic 2, running on the PC, is a great number cruncher. In most forms of Basic numbers are divided into two types - integers (whole numbers, usually in the range -32768 to +32767) and real numbers (very large numbers, and those with decimal fractions) - and it is up to the programmer to specify which type is to be used. Because of the way that computers handle numbers, arithmetic operations are much faster with integers than with reals, and they take up less memory space. Integers are therefore used wherever possible, but often you have to use a real number variable just in case it is needed.

In Basic 2, the programmer does not have to bother about the type of number to use - the computer will decide which type is most appropriate. This ensures that numbers are always handled with optimum efficiency, as well as making programming simpler.

If you need to do any calculations, outside of a program, or want to test a formula, then type **PRINT expression** in the Dialogue screen. Complex expressions are evaluated from left to right, but in order of precedence; *powers* are calculated first, then multiplication and division, followed by addition and subtraction. If brackets are used then the calculations in these are performed before the overall sum is tackled. E.g. the command:

PRINT 2 + 4 * 12 / (8 - 2) + 3^2

evaluates in this order:

(i) 2 + 4 * 12 / 6 + 3^2
(ii) 2 + 4 * 12 / 6 + 9
(iii) 2 + 48 / 6 + 9
(iv) 2 + 8 + 9
(v) 19

Calculations are performed within Basic following exactly the same rules. They may include any of the arithmetic functions; trigonometry - all Sines, Cosine and Tangent functions are present (see Section 17); rounding to whole numbers - in several different ways; roots, powers and logs; and two simple, but useful, statistical functions - MIN and MAX. These find the smallest and largest values in given lists.

■ SECTION 8
Number crunching

The following short program will draw together some of the ideas covered so far, to produce a 'calculator' which is almost as effective - if not as pretty - as the one that you can call up from the BASIC2 menu. You can put in a sequence of signs and numbers, and it will work out a running total. (It therefore does not work in the same way that Basic would evaluate an expression.)

```
REM the calculator
WINDOW #1, FULL ON
CLS #1
LABEL new_sum
INPUT "First Number ";num
INPUT "Sign + - * / = ";sign$
WHILE sign$ <> "="
INPUT "Next number ";nex
IF sign$ = "+" THEN num = num + nex
IF sign$ = "-" THEN num = num - nex
IF sign$ = "*" THEN num = num * nex
IF sign$ = "/" THEN num = num / nex
PRINT "Current value = ";num
INPUT "Sign + - * / = ";sign$
WEND
LABEL print_out
PRINT "The answer is ";num
INPUT "Another ";answer$
IF UPPER$(answer$) = "y" GOTO new_sum
END
```

Number crunching

```
  File  Program  Edit  Fonts  Colours  Patterns  Lines  Windows      BASIC2
┌─────────────────────────────────────────────────────────────┐
│ H │                       Results-1                           │
│First Number?23                                                │
│Sign + - * / = ?+                                              │
│Next number?20                                                 │
│Current value =  43                                            │
│Sign + - * / = ?/                                              │
│Next number?5                                                  │
│Current value =  8.6                                           │
│Sign + - * / = ?=                                              │
│the answer is  8.6                                             │
│Another ?y                                                     │
│First Number?12                                                │
│Sign + - * / = ?*                                              │
│Next number?4                                                  │
│Current value =  48                                            │
│Sign + - * / = ?=                                              │
│the answer is  48                                              │
│Another ?n                                                     │
│                                                               │
│                                                               │
│                                                               │
└─────────────────────────────────────────────────────────────┘
```

Calculator

■ SECTION 9
Program structure

A short program can be treated as a simple sequence of commands - which may or may not loop or branch, but as the program gets longer and more complicated, you need to think in terms of structure.

The best way to plan a program is to see it as a set of routines, each consisting of a number of lines that together perform a distinct part of the operations. As far as possible, each routine should be developed and tested separately - though keeping the overall design in mind. It is much easier to isolate, and to cure errors (or *bugs*) this way. It is also possible to plan the structure of the program, without getting bogged down in details.

Suppose you wanted to create your own paintbox program - having decided that you need something better than GEMPaint (!). If you simply sat down at the keyboard and started to program it in one line at a time, you would soon be in a mess. It might work, at the end of the day (or week, or month), but it would be a very tangled program. What you should do is plan it, on these sort of lines:

    Title page
    Set up windows and screens
    Offer draw options
        - point
        - line
        - circle
        - box
    Change colours, styles?
    Check for exit, otherwise loop back to options

Now you can see the things that must be done first. The title page can obviously wait until later, and initially you do not need all of the options. What is important is that you get the windows set up properly, and that you have the main option selection routines going. This might include a set of lines like this:

```
....
IF choice$ = "C" GOTO make.circle
IF choice$ = "B" GOTO make.box
....
```

Program structure

As long as there are lines labelled **make.circle** and **make.box**, this routine will work. It doesn't matter that at first the circle routine consists of these three lines:

```
LABEL make.circle
PRINT "Not yet implemented"
GOTO choice.time
```

The full routine can be written later, when you have got the overall shape of the program correct, and have perfected your techniques on the easier drawing routines. (Writing the easier bits first is a very good way to tackle a program. It is good for morale and may also help to solve or simplify some of the problems that you expect to meet later.)

Subroutines

If you have a routine which is needed at several points in the program, then rather than key it in several times, turn it into a subroutine. All this involves is putting a **RETURN** command at the end, and when you want the program to perform it, you call it up with a **GOSUB** rather than **GOTO**. When the program reaches the end of the subroutines and hits the RETURN line, it will jump back to the statement after the GOSUB that sent it there.

Subroutines can be 'nested', so that you can call one up from within another - there is no practical limit to the number of GOSUB jumps that can be performed in succession. The only requirement is that you must leave with a RETURN instruction. If you jump out with a GOTO, then the RETURN addresses get confused, and are left behind to clog up the memory.

Normally, subroutines are used for those actions that are needed several times at different parts of the program. Typical examples are the lines that produce "Press any key to go on" messages, and wait for a keypress; or protected INPUT routines - the sort that make sure that the right sort of data and suitable values are typed in. Using subroutines for these doesn't just save typing and memory space, it also makes it much easier to debug and to alter a program.

■ SECTION 9
Program structure

Sometimes though, people prefer to write their programs as a series of subroutines linked by one main routine. The CONVERT program given later is an example of this type. Here subroutines are used to give a clearer structure to the program. They are the equivalent of *procedures* that are an important part of program design in some versions of Basic and other languages.

■ SECTION 10
Through the window

Basic 2 gives you full control over the GEM windows, although the mouse and **Windows** menu can normally be used as well when Basic programs are running. You can adjust their size, position, nature and select how many, and which, to make visible on your screen.

Each window is linked to a *virtual screen,* all or part of which may be visible at any given time. The screen is managed in memory, so that any alterations that are made to a hidden part of the screen are recorded, and will be seen should that part of the screen be exposed later.

A virtual screen can be set to any chosen size, though it is initially set to the full size, measured in pixels. (A **pixel** is the smallest part of the display - a single dot of light). The number of pixels (horizontal by vertical) depends on your system, as follows:

PC1512	Monochrome	(PC-MM):	640 by 200
	Colour	(PC-CM):	640 by 200
PC1640	Monochrome	(PC-MD):	720 by 350
	Colour	(PC-CD):	640 by 200
	Enhanced	(PC-ECD):	640 by 350

Windows can also be of any size up to the limit of their virtual screen, though smaller limits may be set from Basic. The nature of a screen - whether for text only, or for graphics and text - can also be set.

Screens, and their viewing windows, are linked to numbered *streams* - channels of communication between the program and any external devices such as screens, printers and disk drives. Basic 2 can handle up to 16 streams at once. Stream #0 is usually the printer; #1 and #2 are usually Results screens 1 and 2; a further 2 streams could be linked to screens. The remainder are available for file-handling, as disk files are also addressed through streams.

Before you can use a stream, you must clear the lines of communication with an OPEN command.

OPEN #3 WINDOW 3

Through the window

Windows 1 and 2 are linked to streams #1 and #2 and opened by Basic, as default settings.

When text is printed, or a graphic drawn, the output can be directed to a particular screen by including its stream number in the command line.

PRINT #2, "Text on screen two"
CIRCLE #3, 1000;500,200

If the default screen set-up (ie. with stream #1 as the graphics screen Results-1 , and stream #2 as the text-only Results-2) is not to your liking, then the windows and screens can be reset in your programs.

SCREEN #stream GRAPHICS options
SCREEN #stream TEXT options
SCREEN #stream TEXT options

These define a virtual screen for use with either graphics or text. The options are the same, except that with a FLEXIBLE screen, the screen will adjust to suit any alteration in window size. The first option does not, therefore, apply.

width FIXED, height FIXED sets the size of the screen. If **FIXED** is used, the window's dimensions must be the same as the screen. Thus the line:

SCREEN #1 GRAPHICS 600,200

sets up a graphics screen linked to stream #1, 600 by 200 pixels. This puts no restrictions on the window. To do that, we need to look at other options. The key ones are:

MAXIMUM width, height sets a maximum size for the window
MINIMUM width, height sets a minimum size for the window

eg. **SCREEN #1 TEXT FLEXIBLE MAXIMUM 200,100**

This line would create a text screen with a maximum window size of 200 by 100 pixels.

Through the window

There are a number of commands which allow you to control the window from within Basic, giving the same functions that are available via the mouse in GEM. Of these the most important are:

WINDOW OPEN which makes a window visible
WINDOW CLOSE which hides a window
WINDOW FULL ON/OFF switches between full and current size

The other Window commands are listed in the summary.

Sequences like this can be found at the start of the graphics programs listed later:

SCREEN #1 GRAPHICS 600 FIXED, 200 FIXED
WINDOW #1 OPEN
WINDOW #1 FULL ON

If you type this in and run it as it stands, you won't get much chance to see what happens because Basic will restore the normal four window display as soon as the program ends. Add a GOTO loop, or an INPUT line to hold the display.

Display Modes

There are two components to any screen character or graphic - its foreground colour, or 'ink', and its background, or 'paper'. Normally, any material printed or drawn on the screen will overwrite what was there previously, as both ink and paper are displayed. This is

MODE 1 - *Replace.*
There are alternatives:
MODE 2 is *Transparent,* with coloured ink on clear paper;
MODE 3 is *XOR*, where the ink is XOR'd with the current pixel colour. The effect is that where inked areas overlap the paper shows through.
MODE 4 is *Reverse Transparent,* where background areas are printed in the ink colour, and foreground areas are left clear.

The program MODES explores the display modes.

Points, lines and shapes

That last Section was a heavy one, so let's take a little light relief by exploring some more graphics commands.

PLOT x1;y1,x2;y2 , ...

plots a series of given points. There is no set limit to the number of points that can be plotted by one command. There are, however, practical limits. The command line must not exceed 256 characters, and - a significant consideration - long lines are much harder to debug. Basic will tell you if there is an error in a line, but not whereabouts!

PLOT normally places a dot on the screen, but the keyboard MARKER may be included in the command to select an alternative. The choice is between dot, plus, asterisk, square, cross and diamond, e.g.

PLOT 2000;1000 MARKER 2

This would plot a plus sign at 2000;1000.

The display MODE number and the COLOUR can also be written into the command line. For colours, use the reference numbers that are shown in the **Colours** menu.

PLOT 1000;1000,1500;1250 MARKER 3 COLOUR 2

This will plot two red asterisks. Notice the punctuation on all of these lines. Semi-colon between the x;y values, comma to separate pairs of co-ordinates, and a space between keywords.

If you run a PLOT command through a loop, you can produce solid or dotted lines. Try this:

```
CLS
INPUT "STEP size ";step_size
INPUT "COLOUR number ";col
FOR x = 1000 TO 5000 STEP step_size
PLOT x;2000 COLOUR col
NEXT x
WHILE INKEY$=""
WEND
```

■ SECTION 11
Points, lines and shapes

(The two lines at the end wait for a keypress before allowing the program to end, as the Basic screen will corrupt the display.)

Basic 2 is pleasingly fast in the way that it plots lines, but for a quicker, and easier, means of drawing lines, use this command:

LINE x1;y1 , x2;y2 ,... options

This draws lines linking a series of points. The options that may be written into the line include COLOUR and MODE, but also **STYLE, WIDTH, START** and **END**. If these are used, they must be followed by the reference numbers drawn from the Lines menu.

LINE 1000;1000,4000;1000 STYLE 1 WIDTH 5 START 1 END 1

This draws a thick line with an arrow on each end.

Do you need a grid on your screen so that you can see where to plot and draw? Try this:

```
SCREEN #1 GRAPHICS 600 FIXED, 200 FIXED
WINDOW #1 OPEN
WINDOW #1 FULL ON
FOR x = 0 TO 5000 STEP 100
LINE x;0,x;5000
NEXT x
FOR y = 0 TO 5000 STEP 100
LINE 0;y,5000;y
NEXT y
LABEL hold.it
GOTO hold.it
```

On a PC1640 with monochrome display or ECD the screen is only about half the depth of the actual screen. The y coordinates still range to 5000 and as a result the x coordinates are scaled up to a much larger value. To make fuller use of the screen replace the first line with:

SCREEN #1 GRAPHICS 600 FIXED, 350 FIXED

Points, lines and shapes

Grid for plotting and drawing

Co-ordinate Systems

So far we have used the co-ordinate system set by Basic 2. If you prefer, you can define your own. The command is:

USER SPACE width,height

The x and y coordinates are initially set to 0 to 5000 each way. As even a full size screen is only 640 (or 720) pixels wide, there is some redundancy in these large numbers! The system is used because graphics output may also be to dot-matrix printers or to plotters, and the over-large coordinates can be easily scaled down to suit different outputs. If you are only drawing on the screen, it may be simpler to use **USER SPACE** to set the co-ordinate system to the same size as the screen.

SCREEN #1 GRAPHICS 600, 200
USER SPACE 600

If only one figure is given, that is assumed to be the number of x co-ordinates, and the y co-ordinates will be set to the same scale.

Points, lines and shapes

Therefore on a screen with more pixels all you have to change is the first statement; the co-ordinate system set by the second statement will be scaled accordingly.

Solid Shapes

We met the commands CIRCLE and BOX earlier in Section 3, although at that stage all colour and style selection was all being done via the menus. As you might expect, most of the options that can be used with LINE also apply to these commands. Both CIRCLE and BOX are also able to use the FILL option, to give solid shapes. There are two forms to this:

FILL ONLY

WITH pat-number

The **pat-number** is selected from the **Patterns** menu. If omitted, the current pattern is used. Where **ONLY** is also given, the shape will appear without an outline - the difference can be very noticeable with the more open patterns.

BOX also has the **ROUNDED** option which rounds off the corners and if you only want an arc, rather than a full circle, then the CIRCLE option **PART start,end** can be used. It is similar in effect to the **ARC** command (see Summary of Basic 2 Keywords). For a CIRCLE PART, the **start, end** figures are given in angles, with 0 being due East.

Perhaps the most flexible of the drawing commands is **SHAPE**. Like LINE, it takes a series of points (at least three), and joins them together. The resulting shape can then be FILLed.

The main problem with **SHAPE** is that you do have to give all of its points - and with a complex shape this can lead to very long lines.

    SHAPE #1, 300;300,400;200,500;300,400;400,300;300 COLOUR 4 STYLE 1 WIDTH 5 FILL WITH 8

Points, lines and shapes

As you can see, graphics commands can easily get large and unmanageable. There are several ways in which you can reduce the scale of the problem. The first is to separate out your colour and style instructions. The command **GRAPHICS options** permits this. Another space-saving device is to hold all commonly used values in variables. In this line, we use **300** five times. If we stored this value in a variable it would lead to a more compact line. Here is that earlier command transformed:

GRAPHICS COLOUR 4 STYLE 1 WIDTH 5 FILL WITH 8
a = 300
SHAPE #1, a;a,400;200,500;a,400;400,a;a

It would now be possible to include a great many more points in the SHAPE command if we needed to.

You can find examples of the graphics commands in many of the programs, but UNDER PRESSURE and CHAMELION offer the best variety.

There are more graphics commands than those given so far, though these are the more important ones. The rest are all outlined in the Basic summary at the back of the book.

■ SECTION 12
Efficient editing

When you are keying in the programs further on in this book, you can save time and energy by making full use of the editing keys and the **Edit** menu.

Edit menu

Typing will normally insert new characters at the current cursor position. If you want to overwrite existing characters, then press the **Ins** key or click the **Insert** line in the **Edit** menu. Either will toggle between **Insert** and **Replace** modes. To delete a character, position the cursor to the right of the one(s) to be erased and use the **Backspace-Delete** key.

The **cursor** can be moved to a new position by dragging it with the mouse, or more simply, by pointing and double-clicking. If you find mouse control inconvenient - as well you might - then the cursor keys can be enabled at the start of a session by pressing CTRL.

■ SECTION 12
■ Efficient editing

To scroll a hidden part of the program list into view, either use the mouse on the right-hand scroller bar, or the up / down cursor keys. For faster movement through a long program, there are four special function keys:

Pg Up - moves up a 'page', or windowful
Pg Dn - moves down a page
Home - jumps to the first program line
End   - jumps to the last line

Lines and Blocks

Basic 2 has the same kind of block editing functions that you would expect to find on a word processor. A line, or set of lines, can be copied, moved or deleted with a few keystrokes. (The functions can be accessed via the **Edit** menu, but the function keys are easier to use in practice.)

f1 marks the start, or the end of a block at the beginning of the current cursor line. A 'block' may consist of a single line.
NB You may only mark one block at a time.

f2 removes any block markers that have been set.

f3 copies a block to slot in at the cursor position.

f4 moves a block to the cursor position - deleting it from its previous place.

f5 deletes the marked block.

If you are going to copy a block of lines to another part of the program and use it - unchanged - there, then don't. Make it into a subroutine instead and call it from wherever you need it. Copying can be a good idea, though, where a similar set of lines is needed further on in a program. It will probably be quicker to edit the block than to type it out from scratch.

Efficient editing

Programs on Disk

You can only have one Basic program in memory at a time, and must remove it with the command **NEW** before starting to key in a new program. But before you do this, **SAVE** the old program on disk by pulling down the **File** menu and clicking that option. The name you give to a program is up to you, subject to certain rules.

1 Filenames can be any combination of letters and digits up to eight characters long. The file-handling system makes no distinction between upper and lower case letters.

2 Hyphens and underline characters may be used, but not spaces.

3 A three-letter extension may be added to the main filename, separated by a dot.

4 For your own convenience, the names used should be meaningful. Names like **PROG-1** and **PROG-2** are to be avoided like the plague. You will have forgotten what they stand for in a matter of days.

Examples of value filenames would be:

SKETCH.PAD
DATABASE
BIRD.PIC

But the following could not be used

MY FIRST includes a space
MR.BROWN'S dot extension too long and includes '
CALCULATOR too long

■ SECTION 13
Pretty printing

This is a rather trivial title for an important step. A screen which uses a selection of styles, sizes and colours of text within a well-planned layout doesn't just look 'prettier', it is also easier to read and to use. If **the things that matter stand out**, then the user is less likely to miss them. Even text-only programs should be displayed on a GRAPHICS screen, unless you particularly need the extra speed or convenience of a TEXT screen.

The appearance of text can be set either by the SET command, or within a PRINT line. The option keywords are the same in either case, but if used with SET, the new values remain in use until reset, while they have only local effects within a PRINT command.

But first, **position**, for *where* text is printed is arguably more important than *how*. The print position can be set by several methods:

> **PRINT AT (column;row);"text"**
> **PRINT TAB (column);"text"**

Here a grid based on the standard character size is used. Columns and rows are numbered right and down, starting at 1,1 in the top left corner of the virtual screen. Where **TAB** is used, the text will be printed at the given column - if it is to the right of the cursor position. If not, it will print at the given column on the next line down.

There are some very good examples of this type of printing in the BUNCO BOOTH program. **AT** is probably the simplest method of positioning text, but for greater flexibility use:

> **MOVE x;y**

This relocates the cursor on the graphic co-ordinate grid. The next string to be printed will have the bottom left corner of the first character at the **x;y** position.

The *angle* at which the text is printed can be changed from the normal horizontal, by the keyword **ANGLE degrees**, where the degrees must be 90, 180 or 270, giving vertical (up or down) and upside-down printing (very good for the Australian markets!)

■ SECTION 13
Pretty printing

Print styles

The variety of FONTS that is available can be easily checked by pulling down the **Fonts** menu. This shows, not merely the names of the fonts, but also the different Point sizes that can be used for the current font. To set these, use either **SET FONT number POINTS size** or include the options in a PRINT command.

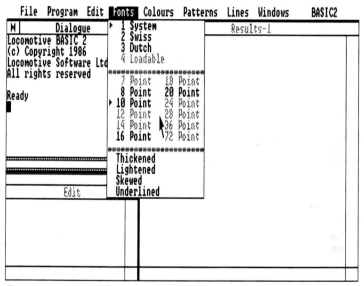

Fonts menu

■ SECTION 13
Pretty printing

The **EFFECTS** option which sets the thickness and style of the text could be easier to manage - but it isn't. Basic 2 permits seven different effects, and they are all controlled by a single byte - or rather by seven bits within that byte. They are all *toggle* switches, which means that if a bit is set to '1' then the effect is turned on, or off, if it is already on.

Bit	Effect
0	thick
1	thin
2	slant
3	underline
4	outline
5	shadow
6	negative

Some examples might help:

Bit 6 5 4 3 2 1 0 toggles 'thick' (0) & 'underline' (3)
Setting 0 0 0 1 0 0 1

Bit 6 5 4 3 2 1 0 toggles 'thin' (1) & 'slant' (2)
Setting 0 0 0 0 1 1 0

The bit setting has to be given as a binary number, so the two examples above would be written:

PRINT EFFECTS &X0001001 ....
PRINT EFFECTS &X0000110 ....

When you want to switch off some effects and switch on others, do it with two separate binary numbers in the EFFECTS command. Using the above example again, you could toggle 'thick' and 'underline' OFF, and 'thin' and 'slant' ON, with this:

PRINT EFFECTS &X0001001, &X0000110 ...

It is not a user-friendly system, but it is not too bad if you take it a *bit* at a time!

Only the most important printing options have been covered here. The others are given in the Basic summary at the back of the book.

■ SECTION 14
Mouse control

It is worth remembering that as Basic 2 runs under GEM, the normal GEM mouse facilities are available. It may also be worth summarising the mouse-window controls at this point.

1 Clicking the top left corner - the bow-tie - will CLOSE the window. In Basic - **WINDOW CLOSE**

2 Clicking the top right corner - the diamond - will toggle the window between full size and its previous size. **WINDOW FULL ON/OFF**

3 Dragging on the top bar, (ie. holding the button down while moving the mouse), will pull the window across the display - though its own virtual screen remains the same. **WINDOW PLACE x;y**

4 Dragging on the bottom right corner will alter the size of the window. **WINDOW SIZE width,height**

5 Dragging on the right hand bar will scroll the virtual screen up or down. **WINDOW SCROLL x;Y**

6 Dragging on the bottom bar will scroll the virtual screen left or right. **WINDOW SCROLL X;y**

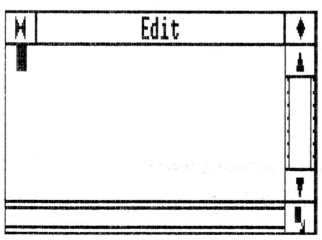

Window showing bars and icons

■ SECTION 14
Mouse control

From Basic you can read the current mouse cursor position, and the button status.

x = XMOUSE
y = YMOUSE

give the x;y position in screen co-ordinates. These will need adjusting if your co-ordinate system is different. If your graphics screen is set to 500 pixels wide, but the x user co-ordinates run from 0 to 5000, then the XMOUSE value will need to be multiplied by 10.

status = BUTTON(number)

This checks the given mouse button (where 1 means left and 2 is right), to see if it is pressed. It also checks the SHIFT, CTRL and ALT keys. The value returned will be -1 if not pressed, 0 if it is, and a higher number if one or more of the keys are also being held down at the time. If *only* the keys are being touched, then the value will be -1.

Add 1 for the right-hand SHIFT key, 2 for the left-hand SHIFT, 4 for CTRL and 8 for ALT. Thus if the value of **status** was 8, it would show that the mouse button and ALT were both being pressed.

In practice, it will usually be enough to check the buttons alone, as few programs will need the extra complications of key presses.

If you want to see an example of the mouse commands in use, look at the ROTATION program.

■ SECTION 15
Turtle graphics

While we are on the subject of animals, let's have a look at Turtle Graphics. These are based on the Logo language that has proved so successful in schools. It gives a simple, but very effective means of drawing on the screen. You can doodle by typing your commands into the Dialogue window, and when you have found a sequence that produces an acceptable design, transfer to the Edit window and key it into a program. If each image is made into a labelled subroutine, then composite designs can be created by calling a sequence of subroutines.

The important thing to remember is that at the end of each operation, whether movement or turn, the cursor is where you left it, and will carry on from there.

To start with turtle graphics, use:

GRAPHICS CURSOR 3 to select the turtle cursor
WINDOW CURSOR ON to make the turtle appear

The key turtle commands are:

FD or **FORWARD number-of-points**

which moves the turtle forward on its current heading, drawing a line. The style of the line can be set by the usual line drawing options:

COLOUR, MODE, STYLE, WIDTH, START and **END**

MOVE FORWARD distance
which moves the turtle without drawing

LT or **LEFT(angle)**
which turns the turtle through a given angle to the left

RT or **RIGHT(angle)**
which turns the turtle through a given angle to the right

■ SECTION 15
Turtle graphics

Working with **Angles in Degrees**, selected from the **Program** menu, and starting with the cursor at 0,0, the following sequence will draw a box in mid-screen.

```
GRAPHICS CURSOR 3
WINDOW CURSOR ON
CLS
POINT 45
MOVE FORWARD 1500
RT 45
FD 1000
LT 90
FD 1000
LT 90
FD 1000
LT 90
FD 1000
LABEL wait
GOTO wait
```

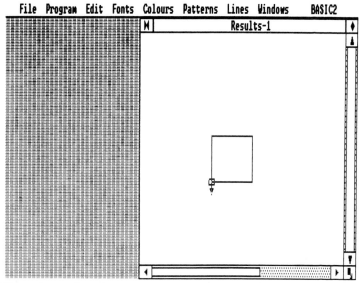

Drawing a box

■ SECTION 16
Data processing

Back in Section 103 you saw how values could be assigned to a variable by the **LET** command. Where a lot of data needs to be transfered to a lot of variables, this can take a lot of typing. A simpler and more efficient method is to **READ** the information from **DATA** lines.

The data to be read is written into lines that start with the keyword **DATA**. Any number of different items may be included in a line, but they must be separated by commas. Strings which include commas, or which have spaces at either end, must be enclosed in double quotes. The only other requirement is that data must be of the right type for the variable into which it is read.

You can see how this works in the following program:

```
PRINT TAB(5);"Name";TAB(25);"Age";TAB(30);"Sex"
FOR times = 1 TO 3
READ name$,age,sex$
PRINT TAB(5);name$;TAB(25);age;TAB(30);sex$
NEXT times
DATA Fred, 27, M, "John Brown", 35, M, "Mrs. Smith", 21,F,
    Jennifer, 16, F
```

A *data pointer* indicates the next item of data to be read. If this routine was run, then at the end, the pointer would be on "Jennifer". The next READ command would use this item. The position of the pointer can be controlled by **RESTORE**. Used by itself, this will move the pointer back to the beginning of the first DATA line in the program - very handy if you want to re-use a set of data. It can also be used in the form:

RESTORE label.name

This moves the data pointer to the named line. A typical application would be where you have a branching program and need to read different sets of data under different conditions. For example, an educational game or quiz might have different sets of questions. At the start of the program you would ask the player to select a topic, then move the data pointer to the appropriate line with **RESTORE chosen.set.name**.

Data processing

Arrays

Where large quantities of data have to be handled - whether it is drawn into the program by READ, LET or INPUT - simple variables are rarely able to cope. If you wanted to collect the personal statistics about 100 people, you could scarcely use sets of variables called person1$, person2$, person3$ .... person100$.The program would be totally unmanageable.

Fortunately, there is a neat solution, and that is to use arrays, These have a common name, but each *element* has a different reference number. Each element of the array can be treated as a simple variable. The simplest type of array has only a single dimension, and can be thought of as a list. So, for instance, if you wanted to store the x and y co-ordinates of 10 points, you could set up two arrays **x(10)** and **y(10)**. The data for these could then be INPUT through a loop:

```
....
FOR num = 1 TO 10
INPUT "x co-ordinate ";x(num)
INPUT "y co-ordinate ";y(num)
NEXT num
```

The size and type of an array has to be defined at an early point in the program, using the form:

DIM name(dimensions) type

This creates an array of the given name, dimensions and type. The rules for the names are the same as for ordinary variables, but note that there is nothing to stop you having an array and a simple variable of the same name - except that it can be confusing.

The number and size of the dimensions is up to you. The x(10), y(10) arrays used above would have been set up with the line:

DIM x(10),y(10)

Data processing

(Really, DIM x(9),y(9) would do for 10 points, as the array elements are normally numbered from 0 rather than 1.)

If you decided to write your own chess-playing program, you could dimension an array to map the board like this:

DIM board(8,8) (or DIM board (7,7))

While a 3-D noughts and crosses game would need:

DIM square(3,3,3)

There is no real limit to the number of dimensions that an array can have! In practice, complex arrays should be avoided as they are difficult to manage and consume large amounts of memory.

Number Arrays

If the **type** is not specified, a number array will take 5 bytes for each element. If the numbers to be stored are integers within certain ranges, then use a suitable type and save memory.

TYPE MEMORY RANGE

TYPE	MEMORY	RANGE		
INTEGER	4 bytes	-2 billion	to	+2 billion
WORD	2 bytes	-32768	to	+32767
UWORD	2 bytes	0	to	+65535
BYTE	1 byte	-128	to	+127
UBYTE	1 byte	0	to	+255

Suppose, for example, that a shop wanted to store the daily sales figures for a dozen assistants, and 10 types of goods over a period of one year, but broken down into weeks. The array then needs four dimensions - 52 weeks, 6 days, 12 assistants, 10 stock lines. If the array is set up by **DIM sales(50,6,12,10)** it will take 50 * 6 * 12 * 10 * 5 bytes - or 180K! You wouldn't be able to find space in memory for it. However, as no assistant is going to sell more than 255 of any stock line in a day, you can use the array type UBYTE. The array now only takes 36K and is relatively manageable.

Data processing

String Arrays

The elements in a string array are normally of variable length, so that **DIM name$(10)** could be used to store 11 names of any length. There is a memory overhead on this as variable length arrays need more management. It will sometimes be more efficient to fix the size of the elements. **DIM name$(10) FIXED 30** allows only 30 characters for each name.

For a fairly complex example of arrays in use, look at the FUNCTIONAL GRID program.

■ SECTION 17
Micro maths

Some of the most spectacular graphics effects are achieved by using the trigonometrical functions - but don't let that put you off if you are not a mathematician, for you can get a long way with just a little understanding.

Let's start by looking at the way that Basic 2 handles angles. It can measure them either in *degrees* - which we all know and love, or *radians* - which computers seem to prefer.

A radian is that angle where the length of the arc is the same as the length of the radius. As the whole circumference of a circle is given by the formula:

2 * PI * radius

this means that there are 2 * PI radians in a full circle; and that one radian is equal to 360 / (2 * PI) degrees - just over 57.

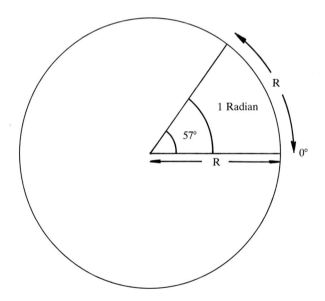

Radians diagram

■ SECTION 17
Micro maths

In both systems, 0 is due East, and the angles are measured anti-clockwise, so that straight up is 90 degrees or PI radians.

If you do not like working with radians - but don't cast them aside too lightly as they do have their advantages - then pull down the **Program** menu and select **Angles in degrees**, or use the Basic command:

OPTION DEGREES

Similarly, **OPTION RADIANS** will switch to the other system.

For a rather dramatic demonstration of the difference between the two systems, get the COILART program running and try it in both.

Sine, Cosine and Tangent

Whichever degree-measurement system is chosen, the trigonometrical functions work in the same way. They are all based on the relationship between the angles and the ratio of the sides in a right-angled triangle. No matter how large or small the triangle is, for any given angle, the ratios of the sides will always be the same.

SINE = OPPOSITE / HYPOTENUSE
COSINE = ADJACENT / HYPOTENUSE
TANGENT = OPPOSITE / ADJACENT

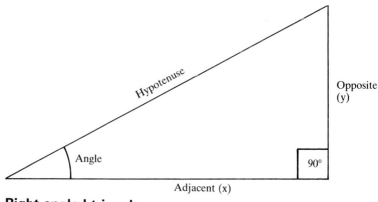

Right angled triangle

In computing terms it means that if you know the distance and bearing of a point, you can work out its x;y co-ordinates. You can use this for plotting a circle. The radius is the hypotenuse, and the bearing of the points go from 0 to 360 degrees. (When the angle goes beyond 90 degrees, either the x or the y or both values are negative.)

```
OPTION DEGREES
FOR angles = 0 to 360
xval = SIN(angles) * 500
x = 2500 + xval
yval = COS(angles) * 500
y = 2500 + yval
PLOT x;y
NEXT angles
```

This will draw a circle, radius 500, at the centre of the screen.

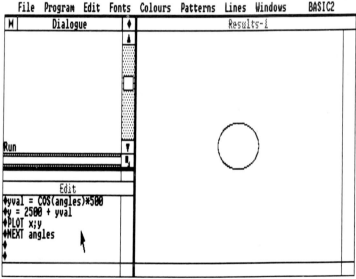

Drawing a circle

Micro maths

You will find examples of the trig. functions at work in STRING and ROTATION. They are rather more complex than a simple circle, but give a good idea of the effects that can be produced by combining the functions in different ways.

Random Numbers

These also have their part to play in producing interesting screen effects, as well as bringing chance into games. Basic 2, like all other Basics, cannot actually produce purely random numbers. Instead, it generates a sequence of *pseudo-random* numbers, by a complex formula, that is so long - over 65000 numbers! - that it can in effect be unpredictable. If you key in and run the MODES program, you will see a series of random boxes appearing at random places on the screen. Wait long enough, and a pattern will begin to emerge - but I defy anyone to predict where the next box will be drawn!

To get a random number, use the form:

var_name = RND(number)

This produces a random (whole) number in the range 0 to number. So that **x = RND(100)** gives you an integer between 0 and 100.

The start-point of the pseudo-random number sequence can be set by:

RANDOMIZE number

You can see the effect of this by typing in and running this routine. Do it several times, and note that the sequence is always the same.

RANDOMIZE 42 - use any value you like here
FOR n = 1 TO 10
PRINT RND(10)
NEXT n

If you just use **RANDOMIZE,** this command will fix the start of the sequence to a value based on **TIME.** Run the routine again and see if you can predict the sequences now.

■ SECTION 18
Strings

Once you have got data into your PC, there is a lot you can do with it, and this applies to strings as much as it does to numbers.

For a start, you can join strings together to make new ones. This is called *concatenation,* and is a very simple process. eg.

title$ = "Mr."
surname$ = "Smith"
firstname$ = "John"
wholename$ = title$ + firstname$ + surname$

This gives the value **"Mr.JohnSmith"** to **wholename$** - and, yes, if you want spaces between the words, you have to add them in as well. The line should perhaps read:

wholename$ = title$ + " " + firstname$ + " " + surname$

Any combination of string variables and literal text (in quotes) can be used in a concatenation.

Another method of producing long strings - though of identical characters - is to use the **STRING$** function.

var-name$ = STRING$(length,character)

The characters can be given directly, or as variables, or as their ASCII codes. e.g.

filler$ = STRING$(10,"*") and **filler$ = STRING$(10,42)**

both make **filler$** equal to **************.

So much for sticking strings together, how about chopping them up. This is generally called *string slicing*. There are several commands that can be used to slice segments off strings. Of these, the most flexible is **MID$,** which is used in the form:

MID$(string,start,length)

The **start** is the number of the first character that you want to slice off. **Length** is optional. If not given, then the end of the string is assumed. This keyword can be used in two ways.

■ SECTION 18
Strings

As a *function* it returns a substring from within another.

a$ = MID$("Amstrad PC",4,4)

gives **a$** the value **"trad"**

As a *command* it transfers a value into the middle of a string. Here the form is:

MID$(string,position)

where a single character is to be assigned, eg. if **word$** held the string *"mistiped"*, then the line:

MID$(word$,5) = "y"

would give the new string *"mistyped"*.

MID$(string,start TO end)

is used where a set of characters is to be assigned to the string. If either **start** or **end** are omitted the ends of the string are assumed.

eg. **MID$("MIDDLE",2) = "U"**

will make the string read **"MUDDLE"**. While . . .

MID$("Newtech Books",5 TO 6) = "is"

gives **"Newtish Books"**.

You can see the MID$ function at work in the UNDER PRESSURE program. This is a version of Hangman, and as such it has to check for the occurrence of the guessed letter in the word. The routine that does the checking takes this shape:

```
FOR n = 1 TO LEN(word$)
IF guess$ = MID$(word$,n,1) THEN ...
NEXT n
```

(Note the use here of the function **LEN,** which gives the number of characters in a string.)

Strings

An alternative way to look for a string within another string is to use the function **INSTR**.

INSTR(start-point,string,string-to-look-for)

This searches through a **string** for the occurrence of the second string - it may be a single character. If the **start-point** is not given, then the search starts at the beginning. The result will be the position of the string within the other - if found - or 0 if it is not there. Look again at UNDER PRESSURE, and you will find a routine there that checks each guess against previous tries. It is based on this:

> **INPUT "Guess a letter ";guess$**
> **tried = INSTR(bad.guess$,guess$)**
> **IF found = 0 THEN PRINT "You've already tried that"**

Concatenation and slicing are important, but only two ways in which strings can be manipulated. You will meet other string functions in the programs, and will find descriptions of them in the Basic summary at the back.

A file is a collection of data, stored on a disk. It will be sub-divided into *records,* each of which will contain one or more *fields.* If you think of a file as a card-index system, then a record is equivalent to a single card, and a field is a line on a card. Files can be handled in several different ways by Basic 2, but at this level, it is best to stick to the simpler *sequential* files.

With these, the records are stored in *sequence,* one after another and can only be accessed by working through from the start of the file. A file can be read or written to, but not both at the same time. This means that if you want to alter the data in a file, you have to read it in, make any alterations, and write it out into a new, updated version.

Before you can write data into a file, you have to open up a stream, as you would to write data on a screen:

OPEN #5 OUTPUT "address"

This creates a new file, called **"address",** linked to stream #5. Data can then be written to it using the form:

PRINT #5, print-items

where print-items are strings or numbers, either directly or in variables. They must be separated by commas. It makes sense to write the whole record in one PRINT line, as that way you can see at a glance the order in which variables have been stored. (This is important later when you come to read the data back in.)

```
REM phone book in
OPEN #3 OUTPUT "phone"
REPEAT
INPUT "Name";name$
INPUT "Tel. Number";num
PRINT #3,name$,num
INPUT "Any more (Y/N)";ans$
UNTIL an$ = "N"
CLOSE 3
```

Notice how the file is CLOSEd at the end of the session. This is essential! When data is PRINTed to a file, it is not sent directly to the disk, but is stored in a buffer in memory first. It is then transferred to the disk when the buffer fills up, or when a CLOSE command is given. If you stop the program without closing your files, any data in the buffer would be lost.

To get data back off the disk, you again need to open a stream to it. The records can then be read back in sequence with the INPUT # command, with all the fields being read into variables in a single line.

```
REM phone book out
OPEN #3 INPUT "phone"
REPEAT
INPUT #3,name$,num
PRINT name$,num
UNTIL EOF
CLOSE 3
```

The thing to notice in this routine is the **EOF** in the UNTIL line. This means End of File. When the special EOF character is read off the disk, the routine will stop.

If you type in and run these routines, then the names and phone numbers that are input with the first, will be printed on the screen by the second. You might like to extend the routines by including more fields in your records, so that addresses, birthdays and other data could be stored. If, having created a file, you want to add more records to the end of it, then this can be done by opening the file for extra output. The form is:

OPEN #stream APPEND filename

There are several other variations in the way that files may be opened, and they are given in the Basic summary.

■ SECTION 19
File handling

Having created disk files, you will need to start thinking in terms of disk management - what files are on a disk, what is in them, how can you get rid of them? The disk directory can be accessed from within a Basic program, though this is only really necessary in a complex file-handling program. For the most part, it is more convenient to access the disk through the Dialogue window. All disk commands have two versions, one for use in the window, the other for use within programs. Only the Dialogue version of key commands are given here, but they are all outlined in the Basic summary.

DEL filename

will delete a file from a disk. *Wildcards* may be used in the filename. These are special characters "*" and "?" which can be used to stand for any others. "*" refers to any set of characters. "?" stands for any single character. Thus **DEL "*.BAK"** will delete any file with a ".BAK" extension to its name. **DEL "SO???.*"** would delete any file where the name was five letters long and started with "SO". Use wildcards with care. **DEL "*.*"** will wipe a directory clear.

DIR filename

DIR by itself will list the files in the current directory. If a filename is given, the command will only list those files that meet the specifications - noting that wildcards may be used. So

DIR " *.BAS"

will list all the .BAS files that it finds.

TYPE filename

will print the contents of the named file in the Dialogue window. Wildcards may not be used with this command.

■ SECTION 20
Errors and how to cure them

What an optimistic title! Would that there were a simple method of curing all programming errors! There isn't, though there are ways of reducing the number of errors in your programs, of locating and identifying them, and of curing some of them. But in the end, getting all of the bugs out of a program is a matter of dedication, discipline and hard work.

The simplest errors to spot and cure are those caused by mistyping. Avoid these by always typing in lower case. Basic keywords are automatically converted to upper case when you finish a line, or move the cursor off it. If the keywords are still in lower case then you should spot it at that point. You should also notice if any of your variable names have been converted to upper case. If they have, it means that you have used a keyword for a variable, which is not permitted.

So, check your lines after typing. That will take care of nearly half of the potential errors.

A second source of error is when the values of number variables in a program go beyond their limits while the program is running. The problem is not with the variables themselves - they can cope with any size of number - but with how they are used. If they are being used to calculate graphics positions for a screen display, the values may go beyond the screen co-ordinates. If they are the reference numbers for arrays, they may go beyond the maximum dimension of the array.

If the problem revolves around a *Number out of range* or similar error, then put extra lines in your program to print out the values of relevant variables (perhaps in another window) while the program is running. When it crashes to a halt, you can compare the current values with the possible ranges that they should have, and track back from there to the point where they go out of range.

■ SECTION 20
Errors and how to cure them

When an error causes a program to stop, the edit window will reappear with the cursor at the start of the line containing the error. If, having studied the line carefully, checked the punctuation, made sure that the right variables have been used, and that you really do mean to use the commands that the line contains - if, having done all this, you still cannot identify the problem, then try cutting the line into a set of smaller ones. Take each step one at a time, and the position of the error will become that much clearer. Once you know where it is, there is more hope of solving it.

If the program does not seem to be flowing in the right way, then add lines at the start of routines to print out the routines' label-names on the screen as they are used. That way you can see where the program is going, and check it against your plan. (You did draw up a design before you started programming didn't you? Because if you didn't, then debugging will take far longer. If you don't know exactly what the program is supposed to do, how will the PC know?)

There are also several commands that can help with debugging.

ERR gives the number of the error that caused the crash. The numbers are not very meaningful unless you have a list of errors and their numbers to hand, but you can find the error message by using the form:

PRINT ERROR$(ERR)

If you do want a list of the error messages, then run this program:

```
errnum = 0
REPEAT
PRINT ERROR$(errnum)
errnum = errnum + 1
UNTIL ERROR$(errnum) = ""
```

All of these things will help to identify and cure programming errors, but there will be times when every single command is working perfectly, yet the program still fails to do what it is supposed to do. The problem then is in the design, and you must go back to the original design and work through its logic stage by stage. Put yourself in the position of the computer and try to follow the sequence of events. Try also to see how different parts of the program affect each other.

At the end of the day, there is no substitute for good design. If, when you start on a new program, you resist the temptation to start keying lines in until you have developed a detailed program on paper, then you will be far more likely to produce a successful program, and will spend far less time debugging.

When a program is fully developed, you may want to make sure that the user cannot do anything that would cause the computer to crash. This can be managed by the command:

ON ERROR GOTO label-name

This line prevents the crash, and re-directs the program to a named error-handling routine. The routine may simply start the program off again from the first line, or take more organised action on the basis of the error number. To restore normal error -handling, use:

ON ERROR GOTO 0

You can also prevent people from breaking into a program while it is running by using the command

OPTION RUN

This will protect the program or a single routine within it by disabling Break and STOP. It doesn't just protect your valued routines from prying eyes, it also saves the user from problems that could be caused by accidentally pressing CTRL and C, or clicking the STOP line in the Program menu. To re-enable breaks, use:

OPTION STOP

Good luck and happy Basic 2 programming.

PART TWO

Programs

■ SECTION 21
Art

When keying in these listings, look out for lines starting two spaces in from the left, as below.

```
PRINT POINTS (10) COLOUR(4); AT(22;1);LEFT$(m$,n/40); COLOUR (1);":-";CHR$(8);
  CHR$(8);" ";
```

This means that the line is a continuation of the line above, and that you **SHOULD NOT** press the CARRIAGE RETURN button between the two. This precaution is necessary because Basic2 does not have the line numbers usually used to show the beginning of a new line.

PC1640 displays
If you have an Amstrad PC1640 with monochrome or ECD display you will have to adjust any statements that set the screen size according to the number of pixels. Most of the programs following start with the command:

SCREEN #1 GRAPHICS 600 FIXED, 200 FIXED

This should be changed to one of the following:

SCREEN #1 GRAPHICS 640 FIXED, 350 FIXED (PC-ECD)

or

SCREEN #1 GRAPHICS 720 FIXED, 350 FIXED (PC-MD)

There is no need to change the USER #1 or other graphics statements. Text windows are unaffected since there are 24 rows of 80 columns on all displays (unless you change the font, of course).

Coilart

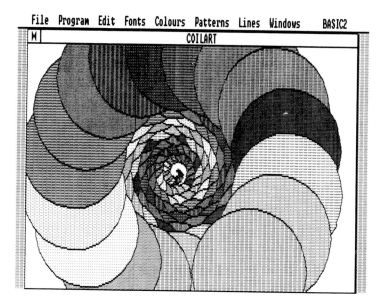

This program is very simple. It draws filled circles (with black outlines to separate the circles) around the points of an ever increasing circle.

Some interesting effects can be achieved by doing combinations of the following:

Change the value of the MODE statement to either 2 or 3.

Change the value of the FILL WITH command (between 0 and 31)

Change the value of STYLE to select a variety of lines

```
REM*** set up a full graphics screen ***
CLOSE #1
CLOSE #2
OPEN #1 WINDOW 1
```

■ SECTION 21
Art

```
SCREEN #1 GRAPHICS 600 FIXED, 200 FIXED
WINDOW #1 OPEN
WINDOW #1 FULL ON
c = RND(15):REM*** initialise colour ***
FOR n = 0 TO 2670 STEP 20

REM*** compute positon around the circle ***
z1=SIN(RAD(n))
z2=COS(RAD(n))
a=n*1:REM*** alter this ratio to change the size of the coil ***

REM*** draw filled circle ***

REM*** change STYLE, FILL WITH, line COLOUR and MODE for wild effects ***
CIRCLE 3500+a*z1;2400+a*z2,n/2 COLOUR c FILL WITH  4 MODE 1

REM*** draw black outline to circle ***
CIRCLE 3500+a*z1;2400+a*z2,n/2 COLOUR 1 STYLE 1

REM*** change colour ***
c = c + 1: IF c = 16 THEN c = 1

NEXT n

REM*** waits until a key is pressed before ending program ***
LABEL fin
IF INKEY$ = "" GOTO fin
STOP
```

Modes

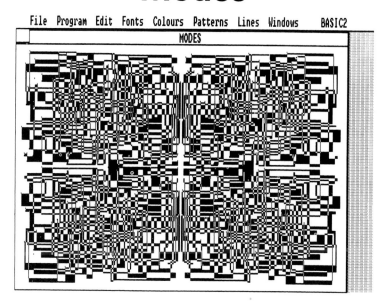

This program has very simple calculations — it simply places random boxes around the screen, mirroring the box about the centre of the screen both horizontally and vertically. This may not seem very exciting, but the whole point of the program is for you to experiment with different values of MODE, FILL WITH (patterns), COLOUR, STYLE (line type) and WIDTH.

You may also like to include some random circles with random radii.

```
REM*** set up screen ***
CLOSE WINDOW 3
CLOSE WINDOW 4
SCREEN #1 GRAPHICS 600 FIXED,200 FIXED
USER #1, SPACE 600,400
WINDOW #1, TITLE "MODES"
CLS #1
```

```
REM*** main loop ***

LABEL loop

REM*** select random size ***
siz = RND (60)+60

a = RND(3)

REM*** select random position within quarter of the screen ***
x= RND(320-siz)-30:y= RND(220-siz/a)-30

REM*** draw top right box ***
BOX #1, 300+x;200+y,siz,siz/a MODE 3 COLOUR RND(15) FILL WITH 8 STYLE 1 WIDTH 1

REM*** draw bottom right box ***
BOX #1, 300+x;200-y-siz/a,siz,siz/a MODE 3 COLOUR RND(15) FILL WITH 8 STYLE 1
  WIDTH 1

REM*** draw top left box ***
BOX #1, 300-x-siz;200+y,siz,siz/a MODE 3 COLOUR RND(15) FILL WITH 8 STYLE 1
  WIDTH 1

REM*** draw bottom left box ***
BOX #1, 300-x-siz;200-y-siz/a,siz,siz/a MODE 3 COLOUR RND(15) FILL WITH 8 STYLE
  1 WIDTH 1

GOTO loop
```

Art

Plank

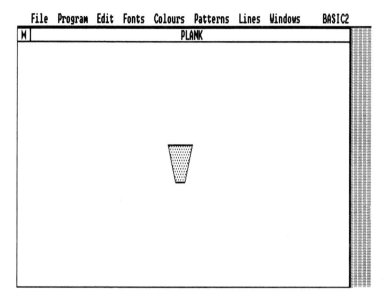

File Program Edit Fonts Colours Patterns Lines Windows   BASIC2

The picture above does not do much for this program, but once you run it you may become a little more interested.

The program uses just two simple loops to spin the plank through 180 degrees twice. The second spin is drawn in grey to strengthen the illusion of movement — change this to white and see the difference.

```
REM*** set up screen ***
CLOSE WINDOW 3
SCREEN #1 GRAPHICS 600 FIXED,200 FIXED
USER #1, SPACE 600,200
WINDOW #1, TITLE "PLANK"

LABEL loop
```

```
REM*** spin plank and display white side ***
FOR n = 1 TO 50 STEP 10
s=n/5

REM*** draw shape ***
SHAPE #1, 300+s;100+n,290-s;100+n,270+s;100-n,320-s;100-n,300+s;100+n

GOSUB wait:REM*** delay to equalise spin rate of white and grey views ***

REM*** erase shape ***
SHAPE #1, 300+s;100+n,290-s;100+n,270+s;100-n,320-s;100-n,300+s;100+n COLOUR(0)

NEXT n

REM*** spin plank and show grey view ***
FOR n = 45 TO 6 STEP -10
s=n/5

REM*** draw shape ***
SHAPE #1, 270+s;100+n,320-s;100+n,300+s;100-n,290-s;100-n,270+s;100+n  FILL
   WITH 1

REM*** erase shape ***
SHAPE #1, 270+s;100+n,320-s;100+n,300+s;100-n,290-s;100-n,270+s;100+n COLOUR(0)
   FILL WITH 8
NEXT n

GOTO loop

LABEL wait
FOR a = 1 TO 250:NEXT a
RETURN
```

Waiting Room

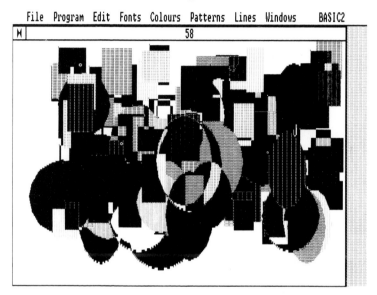

This program imitates those useless screens you get in the waiting rooms of some more upmarket dentists and doctors, which far from relaxing most people, bring on an attack of nausea.

There's little else I can say about this program, except that by changing the value of MODE you can alter the overall appearance of the image created.

```
REM*** set up screen ***
CLOSE WINDOW 2
CLOSE WINDOW 3
SCREEN #1 GRAPHICS 600 FIXED,200 FIXED
USER #1, SPACE 600,200
CLS #1

REM*** main loop ***

LABEL loop
```

Art

```
REM*** select random colour ***
GRAPHICS COLOUR (RND(13)+2)

REM*** select random size ***
sizx = RND (30)+30:sizy= RND (20)+20

REM*** select random position, depending upon size ***
x= RND(590-2*sizx)+sizx:y= RND(190-2*sizy)+sizy

REM*** occasionally draw an ellipse ***
IF RND(10) >8 THEN ELLIPSE #1, x;y,sizx,sizy/sizx MODE RND(4) COLOUR(RND(15))
    FILL WITH 8

REM*** draw box ***
BOX #1, 600-x;200-y, sizx,sizy FILL WITH 8 MODE RND(4)

REM*** display x position in the title bar for extra interest ***
WINDOW #1, TITLE STR$(x)
GOTO loop
```

Spiro

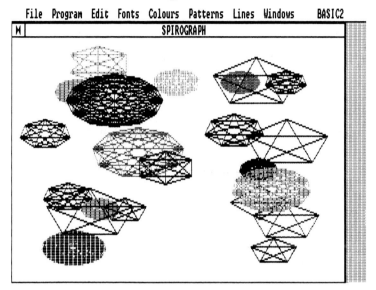

File Program Edit Fonts Colours Patterns Lines Windows   BASIC2

SPIROGRAPH

This program uses simple trigonometry to produce polygons with all their corners joined. It might be interesting to combine this program with the MODES program.

```
REM*** set up screen ***
CLOSE WINDOW 3
CLOSE WINDOW 4
WINDOW #1, TITLE "SPIROGRAPH"
SCREEN #1 GRAPHICS 600 FIXED,200 FIXED
USER #1, SPACE 600,400
CLS #1

REM*** main loop ***

LABEL loop
```

■ SECTION 21
Art

```
REM*** SELECT RANDOM COLOUR ***
 GRAPHICS COLOUR (RND(13)+2)

REM*** select random size ***
siz = RND (60)+30


REM*** select random position ***
x= RND(600-siz*2)+siz:y= RND(400-siz)+siz/2

REM*** compute number of points on shape ***
steps = RND(3)*RND(4)+3

REM*** draw spirographic polygon ***
FOR n =0 TO PI*2 STEP PI*2/steps
FOR a = 0 TO PI*2 STEP PI*2/steps
LINE #1, x+ siz*SIN(a);y+(siz/2)* COS(a), x+ siz * SIN(n); y+ (siz/2)*COS(n)

NEXT a
NEXT n

GOTO loop
```

Cubes

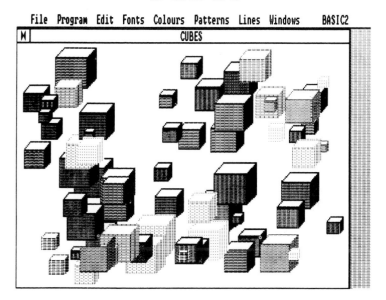

This is an ad infinitum program; it will keep drawing random coloured cubes of random sizes around the screen until the next power cut.

Once the position and size of the cube have been decided, three simple shapes are drawn to represent it. This is how the screen coordinates are calculated:

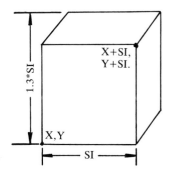

■ SECTION 21
Art

The faces of the cube are filled with different patterns, and by swapping these fill styles you can alter where the light appears to come from.

```
REM*** set up screen ***
CLOSE WINDOW 2
CLOSE WINDOW 3
SCREEN #1 GRAPHICS 600 FIXED ,200 FIXED
USER #1, SPACE 800,600
CLS #1
WINDOW #1, TITLE "CUBES"
WINDOW #1 FULL ON

REM*** main loop ***
LABEL loop

REM*** select random colour ***
 GRAPHICS COLOUR (RND(13)+2)

REM*** select random position ***
x= RND(350)*2:y= RND(250)*2

REM*** select random size ***
si = RND (60)+20

REM*** draw front face ***
BOX #1, x;y, si,si FILL WITH 4 MODE 1

REM*** draw side of cube ***
SHAPE #1,x+si;y,x+si*1.3;y+si*.3,x+si*1.3;y+si*1.3,x+si;y+si FILL WITH 8

REM*** draw top of cube ***
SHAPE #1,x;y-3+si, x+si;y-3+si,x+si*1.3;y+si*1.3, x+si*.3;y+si* 1.3 FILL WITH 0
GOTO loop
```

Functional Grid

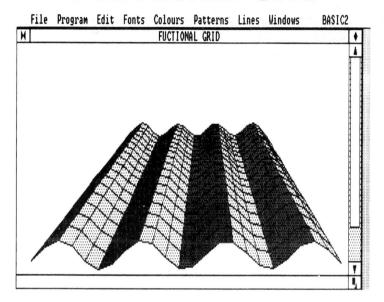

This program produces a true three dimensional perspective view of a function plotted on a two dimensional grid.

The first loop calculates the height of each point of intersection on a grid according to the function given (in this case, Y = SIN(X)-Z). The two screen coordinates of this point are then computed, with the horizontal value (XT) being stored in the HORIZ array, and the vertical value (YT) being stored in the VERT array.

The second loop then steps through these two arrays, and firstly calculates if the part of the grid being drawn is shadowed or highlighted. The shape for this part of the grid is then drawn, filled with the relevant pattern to give the required effect of lighting.

If you wish to change the final image here are a few suggestions:

Change the value of the variable V, which specifies the angle of view.

■ SECTION 21
Art

Use a different function to calculate Y. For instance, Y=INT(SIN(X)-Z) gives an impression of a skyscraper.

```
REM*** set up screen ***
CLOSE WINDOW 2
CLOSE WINDOW 3

REM *** initialize graphics screen ***
SCREEN #1 GRAPHICS 600 FIXED, 200
WINDOW #1, TITLE "FUCTIONAL GRID"
WINDOW #1 OPEN
WINDOW #1 FULL ON

REM*** set up arrays for storing grid points ***
DIM horiz(23,20),vert(23,20)

REM*** v varies the angle of view ***
v=15

REM*** loops for positioning in arrays of points of grid ***
FOR x = -13 TO 10
FOR z = -15 TO 5

REM*** compute height of each grid point ***
y = SIN(x)-z

REM*** compute position of grid point on the virtual screen ***
xt=x/(1-z/v): yt =y/(1 - z/v)
a=x+13:b=z+15

REM*** store screen points in the arrays ***
horiz (a,b) = 3900+240*xt: vert (a,b) =1700+230*yt
NEXT z
NEXT x

REM*** loops for extracting screen positions from the arrays ***
FOR col = 0 TO 22
FOR row = 0 TO 16
```

```
REM*** compute which fill pattern to use to give impression of shading ***
IF vert(col,row)< vert(col+1,row) THEN co = 5
IF vert(col,row)> vert (col+1,row) THEN co =1
IF vert(col,row) = vert (col+1,row) THEN co = 4

REM*** draw segment of the grid ***
SHAPE #1, horiz(col,row);vert(col,row),horiz(col,row+1);vert(col,row+1),
   horiz(col+1,row+1);vert(col+1,row+1), horiz(col+1,row);vert(col+1,row),
   horiz(col,row);vert(col,row) COLOUR(4) FILL WITH co
NEXT row
NEXT col

REM*** continuous loop to prevent the corruption of the screen ***

LABEL finite
GOTO finite
```

Functional Ellipses

File Program Edit Fonts Colours Patterns Lines Windows   BASIC2

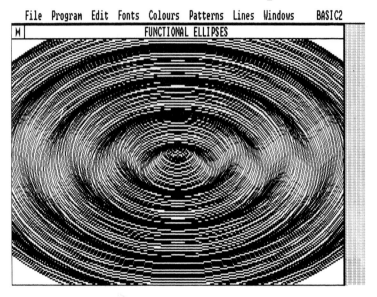

FUNCTIONAL ELLIPSES

This program produces an interesting three dimensional surface by representing a trigonometrical function with ellipses. In the listing you are given, the variable z holds the SIN of the size of the current ellipse. This dictates how far up the screen the centre of the current ellipse is.

The variables height, prox and ratio are used as follows:

Height : The variable z is multiplied by height to give the vertical position of the ellipse centre; the greater the value of height, the higher the peaks and the lower the troughs will appear to be.

Prox : This variable controls how close together the peaks are. The higher the value, the closer the peaks.

Ratio : This controls the ratio of width:height for the ellipses.

Experiment with altering the function used to compute the value of z.

■ SECTION 21

Art

```
REM*** set up screen ***
CLOSE WINDOW 3
SCREEN #1, GRAPHICS 600 FIXED,200 FIXED
USER #1, SPACE 600,200
WINDOW #1, TITLE "FUNCTIONAL ELLIPSES"

REM*** define constants. Change these for different surfaces ***
height = 4
prox = 8
ratio = .3

REM*** draw sequence of ellipses ***
FOR n = 10 TO 400*prox   STEP 10

z= SIN(RAD(n))
ELLIPSE #1, 300;100+(z*height),2+n/prox,ratio
NEXT n

REM*** continuous loop to prevent corruption of the screen ***

LABEL finite
GOTO finite
```

String

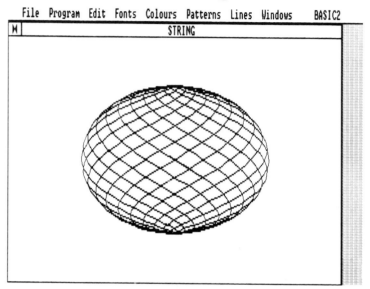

This program has become one of those you see on almost any computer with graphics just to impress passers by.

If however you add COLOUR(RND(15)) to the end of the LINE #1 command, you will get a ball of string in glorious technicolour (well, almost).

The technicolour ball looks best on a grey background. This is achieved by drawing a solid filled box across the whole screen, using the following command:

BOX #1, 0;0,600,200 FILL WITH 8 COLOUR(11)

This must be inserted below the line 'WINDOW #1 FULL ON'.

You can change the colour of your initial background by altering the last value in the BOX #1 command.

■ SECTION 21
Art

For speedier results, increase the value of STEP (0.03 is what we found most effective, as too large a STEP results in a much rougher shape.)

```
REM*** set up screen ***
CLOSE WINDOW 3
SCREEN #1 GRAPHICS 600 FIXED,200 FIXED
USER #1, SPACE 640,600
WINDOW #1, TITLE "STRING"
WINDOW #1 FULL ON

REM*** define loop fo screen positions ***
FOR t = 0.01 TO 31.55 STEP 0.03

REM*** calculate first end of line segment ***
x=320+180*COS(2*(t-0.03))*SIN(2.6*(t-0.03))
y= 300 - 180 *SIN(2*(t-0.03))

REM*** calculate second end of line segment ***
x1=320+180*COS(2*t)*SIN(2.6*t)
y1= 300 - 180 *SIN(2*t)

REM*** draw line segment ***
LINE #1, x;y, x1;y1
NEXT t

REM*** continuous loop to prevent corruption of the screen ***

LABEL finite
GOTO finite
```

Sketch

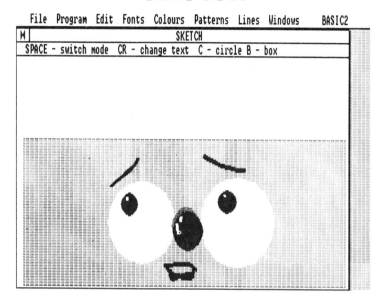

This is a very basic drawing program. It allows you to paint with a line of any colour and thickness, paint with any characters, draw filled boxes and circles, and also clear the screen. The USER #1, SPACE command has been used to set the screen coordinates to the same scale as the mouse coordinates, so there is no need for multiplication of the mouse values to obtain the correct screen position.

While running the program, the colours, patterns, lines and fonts can all be changed by using the menus at the top of the screen.

These are the keyboard controls at your disposal:

SPACE — Switches between the text painting mode and the line painting mode. The mode is displayed at the end of the information line. If painting with text, the text colour in the Colours Menu will be the colour of what you paint.

■ SECTION 21
Art

CARRIAGE RETURN — Pressing this key allows you to input a line of characters (or only a single character if you prefer) from the keyboard. You will not be able to see the characters on screen as you type them, but pressing the CR key once more will secure the characters you have typed. Now when you enter the text painting mode, you will see that the entered text is drawn centred around the arrow. The size, effect and type of text can be altered by use of the top line Fonts Menu.

C — Press the C key to define the centre of your desired circle. You then move the mouse away from this point, and you will see a flickering ellipse move in relation to the arrow. When this ellipse is the desired shape and size, press the left hand mouse button until the circle is drawn. The fill style, colour, line width and line type of the circle can be changed using the top line menus, but this must be done before the circle is drawn.

B — Pressing this key allows you to draw a box. Your position when you press this key becomes the bottom left corner of the box. You must only move up and right of this point to create your desired box, otherwise an error will occur. Press the left hand mouse button once you are happy with the size of your box. Again, you can change the fill style, colour, line width and line type using the top line menus.

Unfortunately, there is no provision for saving and loading images, but if you have loaded your BASIC2 under MS-DOS as opposed to DOS Plus, you will be able to get a printer hardcopy of your picture by pressing the SHIFT and PrtSc keys together (that is if you have a printer, of course).

```
CLOSE #1
CLOSE #2
CLOSE WINDOW 3
OPEN #1 WINDOW 1
WINDOW #1, TITLE  "SKETCH"
REM *** initialize graphics screen ***
SCREEN #1 GRAPHICS 600 FIXED, 200 FIXED INFORMATION ON
OPEN #2, WINDOW 2
```

```
SCREEN #2, TEXT 30 FIXED, 1 FIXED

WINDOW #1 OPEN
WINDOW #1 FULL ON
USER #1, SPACE 600,170
REM *** initialize variables ***
DIM a(200),b(200)
a(1)=0:b(1)=0
count = 2
i$=" SPACE - switch mode  CR - change text  C - circle B - box  "
WINDOW #1, INFORMATION i$
mo$="TEXTLINE"
GRAPHICS WIDTH (1) COLOUR (4):REM *** set colour and line width ***
c$="."
REM *** main loop ***


LABEL loop
x= XMOUSE
y= YMOUSE
IF x <=0 OR x >+600 THEN GOTO loop
IF y<=0 OR y >=170 THEN GOTO loop
ky$=INKEY$: IF ky$="" THEN GOTO moveloop
IF ky$= CHR$(8) THEN CLS #1
IF ky$=CHR$(13) THEN GOSUB change
IF ky$=" " THEN lflag = 1-lflag:PRINT CHR$(7);:WINDOW #1, INFORMATION i$+MID$
   (mo$,4*lflag+1,4)
IF ky$="c" AND bflag = 0 THEN cflag=1:cx=x:cy=y
IF ky$="b" AND cflag = 0 THEN bflag =1:cx=x:cy=y
LABEL moveloop
IF cflag = 1 OR bflag = 1 THEN GOTO shapes
IF BUTTON <> -1 THEN GOTO setpoint ELSE a=x:b=y
LABEL shapes
IF cflag =1 THEN si=2+ SQR(((ABS(x-cx))^2)+((ABS(y-cy))^2)): ELLIPSE #1, cx;cy,
   si,.5 MODE (3) WIDTH(1): IF BUTTON =-1 THEN ELLIPSE #1, cx;cy,si,.5 WIDTH(1)
   MODE (3) ELSE ELLIPSE #1, cx;cy,si,.5 FILL:cflag=0:PRINT CHR$(7);
```

Art

```
IF bflag =1 THEN BOX #1, cx;cy,x+1-cx,y+1-cy MODE (3) WIDTH(1): IF BUTTON =-1
   THEN BOX #1, cx;cy,x+1-cx,y+1-cy WIDTH(1) MODE (3) ELSE BOX #1, cx;cy,x+1-cx,
   y+1-cy FILL:bflag=0:PRINT CHR$(7);
IF BUTTON <> -1 THEN GOTO shapes
GOTO loop
LABEL setpoint
IF lflag = 1 THEN LINE #1, x;y,a;b:GOTO bypass
di = .3*XCELL
MOVE #1, x-.5 * EXTENT (c$);y-di
PRINT MODE (2) c$;
LABEL bypass
a=x:b=y

GOTO loop

LABEL change
REM c$=INKEY$:IF c$="" THEN GOTO change
INPUT #2,c$
RETURN
```

Rotation

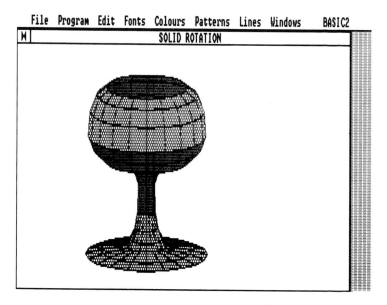

This program allows you to create a three dimensional object from a two dimensional profile.

To define your profile, simply point the mouse cursor at where you want an edge to end and press the lefthand mouse button (holding it down until the line appears). Repeat this until you have the shape you require. You must keep the profile within the inner bounds of the window provided in the bottom left corner, or an error will occur.

Next press the space bar, and the program will enter the drawing procedure.

The greater the steps of rotation entered, the smoother the resultant shape. An ideal value is 20.

Tilt decides the ratio of height:width of the ellipses used to draw the object. Ideal values for tilt lie between 2 and 10.

■ SECTION 21
Art

When the shape is drawn, the program goes throught the two arrays A and B, and extracts the X and Y positions of points on the profile. The Y value dictates how far up the screen the centre of the current ellipse is, while the X value decides how wide the ellipse will be. The height of the ellipse is calculated by dividing its width by the value of TILT.

The loop LP defines the position on the ellipse which the procedure is currently working on. A line is drawn between the current position and the position one step back along the ellipse. Another line is then drawn from the current position to the same current position, but on the next ellipse up.

```
REM*** set up screen ***
CLOSE WINDOW 3
CLOSE WINDOW 4
SCREEN #1 GRAPHICS 250 FIXED, 100 FIXED
WINDOW #1, TITLE"SOLID ROTATION"
WINDOW #1 OPEN
WINDOW #1, PLACE 0,0
REM *** initialize variables ***
DIM a(200),b(200)
a(1)=0:b(1)=0
count = 2
GRAPHICS WIDTH (1) COLOUR (4):REM *** set colour and line width ***

REM *** main loop ***

LABEL loop
x= XMOUSE*12
y= YMOUSE*27

REM *** if a mouse button is pressed, goto setpoint ***
IF BUTTON <> -1 THEN GOTO setpoint
IF INKEY$=" " THEN GOTO drawing
GOTO loop
```

```
REM *** procedure to record point in the a & b arrays ***

LABEL setpoint

a(count)=x
b(count)=y
 REM *** draws line on profile ***
LINE #1, 1.86*x;1.86*y, 1.86*a(count -1);1.86*b(count-1)
count = count +1

LABEL loopone
IF BUTTON <> -1 THEN GOTO loopone
GOTO loop

REM *** input parameters and draw the object ***

LABEL drawing
SCREEN #1, GRAPHICS 600 FIXED,200 FIXED
WINDOW #1, FULL ON
 a(count) = a(count-1)
b(count)=b(count-1)
CLS #1
INPUT #1, "how many steps of rotation ";s
INPUT #1, "factor of tilt is 1:";tilt
INPUT #1, "colour (1 to 15) ";co
GRAPHICS #1, COLOUR(co)
CLS #1
FOR n = 1 TO  count - 1: REM *** loop to specify ellipse drawn ***


FOR lp = 360/s TO 180 STEP 360/s:REM *** loop for points on ellipse ***
q=lp
z1 = SIN(RAD(q)):z2=COS(RAD(q))
z=a(n):z3=z/tilt:z4=3000+a(n+1)*z1
IF z < a(n+1) THEN p1=5:p2=4
IF z > a(n+1) THEN p1=3:p2=5
```

```
 REM *** select fill patterns according to shading required ***
IF ABS(z-a(n+1)) < 20 THEN p1=4:p2=4
IF lp< 90 THEN ff = p2 ELSE ff = p1

REM *** calculate the screen coordinates of the point on the ellipse ***
z5 = SIN(RAD(q-(360/s))):z6=COS(RAD(q-(360/s)))

REM *** draw the ellipse ***

SHAPE #1, 3000+z*z5;700+b(n)+z3*z6, 3000+z*z1;700+b(n)+z3*z2, z4;700+b(n+1)+
   (a(n+1)/tilt)*z2, 3000+a(n+1)*z1;700+b(n+1)+(a(n+1)/tilt)*z2,3000+a(n+1)* z5;
   700 +b(n+1)+(a(n+1)/tilt)*z6 FILL WITH ff
z4=3000-a(n+1)*z1


SHAPE #1, 3000-z*z5;700+b(n)+z3*z6, 3000-z*z1;700+b(n)+z3*z2, z4;700+b(n+1)+
   (a(n+1)/tilt)*z2, 3000-a(n+1)*z1;700+b(n+1)+(a(n+1)/tilt)*z2,3000-a(n+1)* z5;
   700 +b(n+1)+(a(n+1)/tilt)*z6 FILL WITH ff


NEXT lp
NEXT n

REM*** loop to prevent corruption of the screen ***
LABEL finite
GOTO finite
```

Bunco Booth

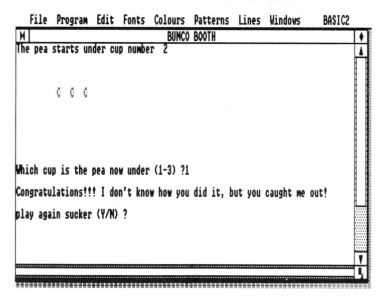

```
File  Program  Edit  Fonts  Colours  Patterns  Lines  Windows      BASIC2
```

This game is based upon the old Bunco Booth con in which a pea is placed under one of three cups, and the punter has to keep his eye on the cup with the pea under it, while the con man switches the cups around at the speed of light.

The program includes some varied comments from the con man. Obviously, as you are typing them in you know the sort of things he is going to say, but if you get someone else to play the game they will no doubt be amused. You can alter the five A$'s for different messages, or add some extra messages — but remember to alter the RND(5) in the guessloop procedure to however many messages you have.

Unfortunately the printing speed of BASIC2 is greatly reduced if large font sizes are used, so the 10 point system font is used. This makes the cups terribly small, but this does increase the difficulty of the game.

```
REM*** set up screen ***
CLOSE #2
WINDOW #1 FULL ON
WINDOW #1, TITLE "BUNCO BOOTH"
SCREEN #1 TEXT FLEXIBLE

REM*** 5 different messages for a correct guess ***
a$ (1)="Congratulations!!! I don't know how you did it, but you caught me out!"
a$ (2)="O.K. smartypants, so you got it right. But I bet it was a fluke."
a$ (3) ="Huh. You think you're clever just cos you got it right this time."
a$ (4)="Damn! You're not supposed to do that!                               "
a$(5) ="I've gotta hand it to you - you sure know how to pull a fast one."

LABEL begin

REM*** draw three cups ***
TEXT CLEAR SCREEN
PRINT #1, COLOUR(4);AT (10;5); "O";AT (13;5);"O";AT (16;5);"O"

REM*** select random cup for the pea to go under ***
pea = RND(3): a(pea)=1
PRINT #1, AT (1;1);"The pea starts under cup number ";pea

REM*** difficulty selection ***

LABEL inloop
PRINT #1, AT(27;12);"        "
INPUT #1, AT (1;12); "level of difficulty (1-20)";l
IF l <1 OR l> 20 THEN GOTO inloop

REM*** move cups a random number of times related to difficulty ***
FOR i = 1 TO l + RND(l)*2

REM*** SELECT random cups to move ***
which =  RND(3)

REM*** goto relevant cup moving routine ***
ON which GOSUB move1,move2,move3
```

```
NEXT i

REM*** input player's guess at where the pea is ***

LABEL guessloop
INPUT #1, AT(1;12);"Which cup is the pea now under (1-3) ";guess
IF guess>3 OR guess<1 THEN PRINT #1, AT(35;12);"        ":GOTO guessloop

REM*** print message (either 1 of 5 success or 1 failure message) ***
IF a(guess) = 1 THEN PRINT #1, AT(1;14);a$(RND(5)) ELSE PRINT #1, AT(1;14);
   "Hah! you're just no darn good!                        "

REM*** option to play again ***

LABEL plloop
PRINT #1, AT(22;16);"            "
INPUT #1, AT (1;16);"play again sucker (Y/N) ";pl$
pl$= UPPER$ (pl$)
IF pl$ ="N" THEN GOTO finish
IF pl$<>"Y"  THEN  GOTO plloop
 GOTO begin

LABEL finish
TEXT CLEAR SCREEN
STOP


REM*** swop cups 1 and 2 ***

LABEL move1
a(0)=a(1):a(1)=a(2):a(2)=a(0)
PRINT #1, AT(10;5); "    "
FOR loop = 0 TO 3
PRINT #1, COLOUR(4); AT(10+loop;4); "0"; AT(13-loop;6); "0"; AT (10+loop;4);
   " "; AT (13-loop;6); " "
NEXT loop
PRINT #1, COLOUR (4);AT (10;5);"0  0"
RETURN
```

```
REM*** swop cups 1 and 3 ***

LABEL move2
a(0)=a(1):a(1)=a(3):a(3)=a(0)
PRINT #1, COLOUR (4); AT(10;5); "   O   "
FOR loop = 0 TO 6 STEP 2
PRINT #1, COLOUR (4); AT (10+loop;4);"O"; AT(16-loop;6);"O"; AT (10+loop;4);
   " "; AT (16-loop;6);" "
NEXT loop
PRINT #1, COLOUR(4); AT (10;5);"O  O  O"
RETURN

REM*** swop cups 2 AND 3 ***

LABEL move3
a(0)=a(2):a(2)= a(3):a(3)=a(0)
PRINT #1, AT(13;5);"    "
FOR loop = 0 TO 3
PRINT #1, COLOUR(4); AT (16-loop;4);"O"; AT(13+loop;6);"O"; AT(16-loop;4);
   " ";AT (13+loop;6);" "
NEXT loop
PRINT #1, COLOUR(4); AT(13;5);"O  O"
RETURN
```

Flasher

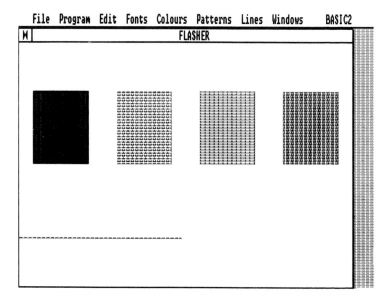

You may be familiar with the idea behind this program — it is based upon that ever popular electronic toy, Simon. It involves memorising a sequence displayed on four coloured lights that flash with an accompanying beep, which has a different pitch for each light. You then have to repeat the sequence, which gets longer until you make a mistake. Simon then says — well, I don't know how to spell it, but he makes a noise of disapproval.

Unfortunately, the beeps on our version are all the same pitch, due to the limited sound abilities of Basic2. To make up for this, a special feature has been added: a red line at the bottom of the screen shrinks as you guess, so if you hang around too long and it disappears, you will lose.

The number keys 1 to 4 on the top row of the keyboard correspond to the four squares on the screen. To set the sequence in motion, just press any key.

Our personal best is 14 events. See if you can beat that.

Games

```
REM*** set up full size graphics screen ***
WINDOW #1, TITLE "FLASHER"
WINDOW #1 FULL ON
SCREEN #1, GRAPHICS 600 FIXED , 200 FIXED
USER #1, SPACE 600,200

REM*** clear screen and draw boxes ***
LABEL startup
CLS #1
FOR n = 1 TO 4
BOX #1, -125+150 * n;100,100,60 FILL WITH (n+3) COLOUR (n)
NEXT n

LABEL loop
IF INKEY$="" THEN GOTO loop

l=1:a$="1"

REM*** MAIN LOOP STARTS HERE ***
LABEL mloop1
a= RND(4):a$=a$+RIGHT$((STR$(a)),1):          REM*** add random No. to a$ ***
l=l+1
FOR n = 1 TO l:          REM*** start loop for whole of sequence ***
ac$ = MID$ (a$,n,1)
ac = VAL(ac$):          REM*** calculate which box to flash ***
GOSUB flash
FOR lo = 1 TO 500:NEXT lo:          REM*** simple delay ***
NEXT n

GOTO guess

LABEL flash

REM*** draw box  in white ***
BOX #1, -125+150 * ac;100,100,60 FILL WITH (ac+3) COLOUR (0)
FOR lo = 1 TO 200:NEXT lo
PRINT CHR$(7);:          REM*** make beep ***
```

```
REM*** draw box in relevant colour ***
BOX #1, -125+150 * ac;100,100,60 FILL WITH (ac+3) COLOUR (ac)
RETURN

LABEL guess
co = 1:timer = 590

REM*** draw full length timer ***
LINE #1, 600;40,0;40 WIDTH(3) COLOUR(2)

LABEL inloop

REM*** decrease timer line & check if time has run out ***
timer = timer -1/2:IF timer < 0 THEN GOTO time_out ELSE LINE #1,600;40,timer;40
   WIDTH(3) COLOUR(0)
an$ = INKEY$:IF an$<"1" OR an$>"4" THEN GOTO inloop
ac= VAL(an$)
GOSUB flash

REM*** checks if wrong key is pressed ***
IF an$<> MID$(a$,co,1) THEN GOTO wrong
LABEL safeloop
 IF INKEY$<> "" THEN GOTO safeloop

REM*** check to see if this is the end of the sequence of guesses ***
co=co+1: IF co> 1 THEN FOR lo = 1 TO 1000:NEXT lo: GOTO mloop1
GOTO inloop

LABEL wrong

REM*** flash boxes random colours and patterns ***
FOR n = 7 TO 1 STEP -1:FOR a=1 TO 4:BOX #1, -125+150 * a;100,100,60 FILL WITH
   (a+3+n) COLOUR (a+n)
NEXT a :PRINT CHR$(7);:NEXT n
PRINT POINTS(15) EFFECTS(1) AT(2;16);"Sorry, that was wrong. You managed ";1-1;
   " events"
```

■ SECTION 22
Games

```
REM*** give option to play again ***
LABEL plloop

INPUT " play again";pl$
IF pl$="n" THEN CLS #1: PRINT POINTS(60) AT(20;20);"GOODBYE"
 IF pl$ ="y" THEN GOTO startup
LABEL wait
IF INKEY$<>" " THEN GOTO wait
STOP
LABEL time_out
REM*** draw wacky line ***
FOR a = 1 TO 3
FOR n = 40 TO 600 STEP 40:LINE #1,n-40;40,n;40 WIDTH(3) COLOUR(2)
NEXT n
FOR n = 560 TO 0 STEP -40: LINE #1, n;40,n+40;40 WIDTH (3) COLOUR(0)
NEXT n

NEXT a

PRINT COLOUR(4) POINTS(12) AT(4;15);"Sorry, you ran out of time. However, you
    managed ";l-1;" events"
GOTO plloop:        REM*** offer play again option ***
```

Reverse

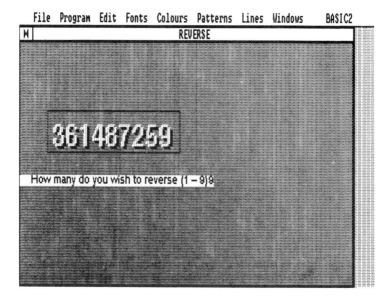

When the program has drawn up a nine digit sequence, it will ask you how many digits you wish to reverse. What you have to do is tell it how many digits from the left you want to reverse, by simply pressing the corresponding number key on the top row of the keyboard.

You then keep reversing until the sequence reads 1 to 9. There is a quick system to solve any sequence, but it might take you a while to work this out.

The program reverses the digits by firstly copying the sequence string into a second string. It then counts through the first string as far as the number being reversed, and replaces each character in the string with the one in the second string positioned at number being reversed + 1 − count.

Games

```
a$="         "

REM*** create random sequence of numbers 1 to 9 ***
FOR n = 1 TO 9

LABEL lloop
p=RND(9)
IF MID$(a$,p,1)=" " THEN MID$(a$,p,1)= RIGHT$(STR$(n),1) ELSE GOTO lloop
NEXT n

REM*** set up screen ***
CLOSE WINDOW 3
SCREEN #1,GRAPHICS 600 FIXED,200 FIXED
USER #1,SPACE 600,200
WINDOW #1, TITLE "REVERSE"
WINDOW #1 FULL ON

REM*** draw patterned background ***
BOX #1,0;0,600,200 FILL WITH 4 COLOUR(14)

REM*** set moves counter to zero and font to 14 point Swiss ***
go = 0
SET #1, FONT(2) POINTS(14)

REM*** main loop ***

LABEL retry
BOX #1,50;108,240,35 FILL WITH 4 STYLE (1) COLOUR(14)

REM*** print sequence in yellow with a dropped shadow ***
MOVE #1,62;112
PRINT POINTS(36) COLOUR(10) MODE (2) ;a$
MOVE #1,58;114
PRINT POINTS(36) COLOUR(6) MODE (2) ;a$

REM*** check to see if sequence is completed ***
IF a$="123456789" THEN GOTO complete
```

```
REM*** ask player how many digits to reverse ***
PRINT:PRINT"    How many do you wish to reverse (1-9)";

LABEL rloop
r$=INKEY$
IF r$<"1" OR r$>"9" THEN GOTO rloop
PRINT r$
r= VAL (r$)

REM*** reverse given number of digits ***
b$=a$
FOR n = 1 TO r
MID$(a$,n,1) = MID$(b$,(r+1)-n,1)
NEXT n
go = go +1
GOTO retry

REM*** message for completing the sequence ***

LABEL complete
PRINT:PRINT "    you solved the sequence in";go;"reversals      "

REM*** loop to prevent corruption of the screen ***

LABEL finite
GOTO finite
```

Chamelion

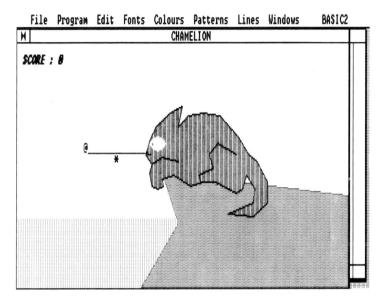

In this game you assume the role of Derek the chamelion. Derek sits all day by the side of the swamp, lapping up passing flies in order to keep up his strength. However, should he flick his tongue out and not catch some lunch, he will waste a bit of strength. If his strength gets too low, he simply will not be able to throw his tongue, and he will starve to death.

Each fly eaten increases Derek's strength, and the stronger he is the further he can throw his tongue. This particular tongue is thrown by pressing any key on the keyboard.

Oh, and if you're one of those few who think Derek looks more like a cat, don't worry — he's having an identity crisis.

```
REM*** set up screen ***
SCREEN #1 GRAPHICS  600 FIXED,200 FIXED
WINDOW #1 FULL ON
```

```
LABEL begin
GOSUB chamelion:REM*** draw chamelion ***
PRINT #1, AT (2;2); EFFECTS(5) "SCORE : 0"

REM*** set up score, fly position, tongue length and tongue ***
sc=0
x=20:y=12
tl = 16
t$="@_____"

LABEL main_loop

REM*** move fly ***
xd= RND(2):yd=RND(2)
IF xd = 2 AND x< 25 THEN x=x+1 ELSE IF x>17 THEN x=x-1
IF yd = 2 AND y< 14 THEN y=y+1 ELSE IF y> 8 THEN y=y-1
PRINT #1, AT(x;y);"*"
MOVE #1,330-(x/3);430-y*2 :PRINT COLOUR(4) MODE (2) ".":REM*** plot eye ***
IF INKEY$ <>"" THEN GOSUB tongue

LABEL caught_return

REM*** blank out fly and eye ***
PRINT #1, AT(x;y);" "
MOVE #1, 330-(x/3); 430 -y*2 : PRINT COLOUR(0) MODE (2) "."
GOTO main_loop

LABEL tongue
tl = tl -.5:IF tl <2 THEN GOTO die:REM*** shorten tongue ***
IF x> (29-tl) AND y= 10 THEN GOTO caught:REM*** check if the fly is got ***

REM*** print tongue ***
FOR n = 2 TO tl STEP 3
PRINT #1, COLOUR(15) AT(30-n;10); LEFT$(t$,n)
NEXT n
FOR n = tl TO 3 STEP -3
PRINT #1,COLOUR(15)  AT(30-n;10);"@"; AT(30-n;10);"   "
NEXT n
```

120

```
PRINT #1, AT(28;10);"  "
RETURN

REM*** kill the fly ***

LABEL caught
tl=tl+1:IF tl=>16 THEN tl  = 16:REM*** lengthen tongue ***

REM*** draw tongue as far as fly ***
FOR n = 1 TO 30-x STEP 2
PRINT #1, COLOUR(15) AT(30-n;10); LEFT$(t$,n)
NEXT n
FOR n = 30 - x TO 2 STEP -2
PRINT #1, COLOUR(15) AT(30-n;10);"∂"; AT(30-n;10);"  "
NEXT n
PRINT #1, AT(28;10); "  "
sc = sc+1
PRINT #1, AT(9;2);EFFECTS (5) ;sc

REM*** blank eye ***
MOVE #1, 330-(x/3); 430 -y*2 : PRINT COLOUR(0) MODE (2) "."
y = 11 + RND(3):REM*** reposition fly ***
GOTO caught_return

LABEL die

REM*** drop tongue ***
FOR n = 1 TO 4: PRINT  COLOUR(15)  AT(29-n;11+n);"∂"; AT(30-n;10+n);"/"
NEXT n

REM*** option to play again ***
PRINT COLOUR(15) AT(25;15);"/" AT(x+1;y-1);"/";AT(x+1;y-2);
  EFFECTS(1) "Hee-Hee!!"
FOR a = 1 TO 9000:NEXT a
PRINT COLOUR(15) AT(x+1;y-2);EFFECTS(1) "Want to play again? (Y or N)"

LABEL again_loop
a$=INKEY$: IF UPPER$(a$)="Y" THEN GOTO begin
```

```
IF UPPER$(a$) <> "N" THEN GOTO again_loop
STOP

LABEL chamelion
CLS #1
USER #1, SPACE 800,700
BOX #1, 0;0,800,200 FILL WITH 8 COLOUR(5):REM*** draw water ***

REM*** draw river bank ***
SHAPE #1, 350;330,800;260,800;0,300;0,390;180 FILL WITH 4 COLOUR(14)
f=500:t=300:g=380

REM*** draw green silhouette of chamelion ***
GRAPHICS COLOUR(11)
SHAPE #1, 310;380,320;420,335;460,370;500,400;520,390;460,415;490,450;500,490;
    490,535;430,560;380,580;360,605;300,605;240,570;200,510;210,570;240,575;280,
    555;320,545;280,530;270 FILL WITH 8
SHAPE #1,480;300,450;300,420;290,380;320,350;310,355;290,340;280,325;290,320;
    330,325;350,310;380 FILL WITH 8

REM*** draw black outline of chamelion ***
GRAPHICS COLOUR(1)
SHAPE #1, 310;g,320;420,335;460,370;f,400;520,390;460,415;490,450;f,490;490,
    535;430,560;g,580;360,605;300,605;240,570;200,510;210,570;240,575;280,
    555;320,545;280,530;270,480;t,450;t,420;290,g;320,350;310,355;290,340;280,
    325;290,320;330,325;350
CIRCLE #1, 340;410,20 FILL WITH 8 COLOUR(0):REM*** draw eye ***

REM*** outline legs ***
LINE #1, 325;350,350;370,390;360 COLOUR(1)
LINE #1, 445;300,440;320,475;340,465;380,485;410,530;380 COLOUR (1)

REM*** draw mouth ***
LINE #1, 310;382,322;378 COLOUR(1)

RETURN
```

Under Pressure

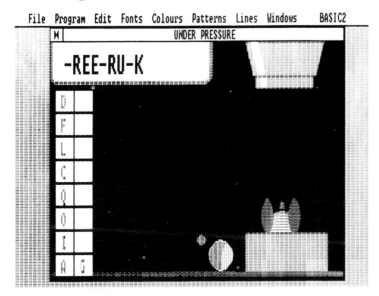

That's what you will be if you're no good at this hangman type game. The computer will display the mystery word as a line of hyphens in the top left of the screen. You simply press the letters which you think might be in the word. If you get a letter right, it will be filled in on the line of hyphens.

If you get a letter wrong, the letter will be displayed in the rack on the left, and the pressure of the Pneumatic Press on which you are lying will be increased (this is displayed on the yellow gauge on the grey control panel). If you get 16 letters wrong, then — well, I'll let you find that out for yourselves.

If you wish to add more words to the computer's list, simply change the number at the beginning of the data to the number of words in the list, and add your words to the end of the data.

```
REM*** set up screen ***
SCREEN #1, GRAPHICS 530 FIXED, 170 FIXED
CLOSE WINDOW 2
CLOSE WINDOW 3
CLOSE WINDOW 4
USER #1,SPACE 600,200
WINDOW #1, TITLE"UNDER PRESSURE"
WINDOW #1, PLACE 65,16

REM*** draw screen ***
BOX #1,0;0,600,200 COLOUR 1 FILL WITH 8

BOX #1, 0;165,330,50 ROUNDED COLOUR 0 FILL WITH 8
BOX #1,0;165,330,50 ROUNDED COLOUR 4 WIDTH 7

BOX #1,250;0,130,45 ROUNDED COLOUR 8 FILL WITH 8
ELLIPSE #1,270;30,10,:5 COLOUR 11 FILL WITH 8
ELLIPSE #1, 310;30,10,.5 COLOUR 2 FILL WITH 8
ELLIPSE #1, 350;18,25,.5 COLOR 6 FILL WITH 8

SHAPE #1, 400;200,560;200,545;170,415;170 COLOUR 4 FILL WITH 4
BOX #1, 420;160,120,10 COLOR 4 FILL WITH 4
SHAPE #1, 410;200,425;200,440;172,425;172 COLOUR 0 FILL WITH 8
BOX #1, 430;161,15,8 COLOUR 0 FILL WITH 8

ELLIPSE #1, 475;53,7,1.7 COLOUR 14 FILL WITH 4
ELLIPSE #1,475;47,30,.3 COLOUR 14 FILL WITH 4
ELLIPSE #1, 475;44,33,.3 COLOUR 2 FILL WITH 4
ELLIPSE #1, 445;50,12,1.4 COLOUR 5 FILL WITH 8
ELLIPSE #1, 500;50,12,1.4 COLOUR 5 FILL WITH 8

BOX #1, 400;0,170,38 COLOUR 4 FILL WITH 4

BOX #1,0;0,600,5 COLOUR 5 FILL WITH 8
BOX #1, 10;0,79,160 COLOUR 6 FILL WITH 8
FOR n = 0 TO 140 STEP 20
BOX #1, 10;n,40,20 COLOUR 2
BOX #1, 50;n,40,20 COLOUR 2
```

```
NEXT n

REM*** define strings and variables ***
READ a
FOR l = 1 TO RND(a-1)
READ a$
NEXT l

REM*** a$ is mystery word, b$ is letters wrong, c$ is word guessed ***
a$ = UPPER$(a$)

b$=""
c$=""
FOR l = 1 TO LEN(a$): c$=c$+"-":NEXT l

PRINT #1, EFFECTS (0) POINTS (20) AT(4;3);c$

wron = 0

REM main letter input loop ***
LABEL wait
ky$ = UPPER$(INKEY$)
IF ky$="" THEN GOTO wait

REM*** check to see if guessed letter has already been tried ***
fl = INSTR(b$,ky$)
IF fl <> 0 THEN PRINT AT (2;1);"You've already tried that.":FOR a = 1 TO 4:
   PRINT CHR$(7);: NEXT a:PRINT AT(2;1);"                    ":GOTO wait

REM*** check if guessed letter is in mystery word ***
fc = 0
FOR n = 1 TO LEN(a$)
IF MID$(a$,n,1) = ky$ THEN MID$(c$,n,1) = ky$:fc=1
NEXT n
PRINT #1, EFFECTS(0) POINTS(20) AT(4;3); c$
IF fc = 0 THEN GOSUB wrong
IF c$ = a$ THEN GOTO complete
```

125

```
GOTO wait

REM*** add wrong guess to list and check for all guesses used ***

LABEL wrong
b$=b$+ky$
wron =wron + 1
ELLIPTICAL PIE #1, 350;18,24,.5,PI*1.5 -(wron*(PI/8)),PI * 1.5 COLOUR 2 FILL WIT
IF wron < 9 THEN MOVE #1, 20;-16+20*wron
IF wron > 8 THEN MOVE #1, 60;-176+ 20*wron
PRINT #1, EFFECTS (0) POINTS (16) COLOUR (4) MODE (2) ; ky$;
IF wron = 16 THEN ELLIPSE #1, 350;18,24,.5 COLOUR 2 FILL WITH 8: GOTO killed
RETURN

REM*** routine to kill player ***
LABEL killed
MOVE #1, 400;70
PRINT #1, POINTS (20) MODE (2) COLOUR (0); "UH - OH!!"
ELLIPSE #1, 270;30,10,.5 COLOUR 0 FILL WITH 8
PRINT CHR$(7);
ELLIPSE #1, 270;30,10,.5 COLOUR 11 FILL WITH 8
MOVE #1, 400;70
PRINT #1, POINTS (20) MODE (4) COLOUR (1) ;"        "
FOR n = 149 TO 39 STEP -11
BOX #1, 425;n,110,159-n COLOUR 1 FILL WITH 4
BOX #1, 440; n+1,15,157 -n COLOUR 0 FILL WITH 8
NEXT n

DIM a(5)
FOR n = 1 TO 30
a((n MOD 5)+1) = a((n MOD 5)+1)+RND(5)
SHAPE #1,400;38,570;38,570-RND(5);38-a(5),536-RND(5);38-a(4),502-RND(5);38-
   a(3),470-RND(5);38-a(2),436-RND(10);38-a(1) COLOUR 2 FILL WITH 8
NEXT n

PRINT #1, EFFECTS(0) POINTS(20) AT(4;3);a$
GOTO finite
```

```
REM*** routine for completion of the mystery word ***

LABEL complete
MOVE #1,400;70
PRINT #1, POINTS(20) MODE(2) COLOUR(0);"HOORAY!!!"

REM*** continuous loop to prevent corruption of the screen ***

LABEL finite
GOTO finite

REM*** list of mystery words, starting with number of words ***
DATA 10, "market","computer","amstrad","treehouse","warehouse","treetrunk",
   "shotgun","wedding","toaster","bicycle"
```

Income Tax

File Program Edit Fonts Colours Patterns Lines Windows   BASIC2

```
M |                    INCOME TAX

     Tax Rates 1986 - 1987

          1 - 17200      29%

          17201 - 20200    40%

          20201 - 25400    45%

          25401 - 33300    55%

          33301 - 41200    60%

     what is your gross income?8500

   What are your total allowances?2300

        Tax due = £ 1798
```

To use this program, simply enter your income and allowances, and you will be told how much tax you owe. The rates are for the financial year of 86/87.

```
REM *** set up screen ***
CLOSE WINDOW 3
SCREEN #1 GRAPHICS 600 FIXED,200 FIXED
WINDOW #1, TITLE "INCOME TAX"

REM*** display tax rates ***
PRINT
PRINT COLOUR (2) POINTS (20)  ;"    Tax Rates 1986 - 1987 "
SET #1, COLOUR (4) POINTS (12)

PRINT:PRINT TAB(20);"1 - 17200 "; TAB(35);"29%"
PRINT: PRINT TAB(18);"17201 - 20200";TAB (37);"40%"
PRINT:PRINT TAB(18);"20201 - 25400"; TAB(37);"45%"
```

```
PRINT:PRINT TAB (18);"25401 - 33300"; TAB(37);"55%"
PRINT:PRINT TAB(18);"33301 - 41200"; TAB (37);"60%"

REM *** Tax constants ***
b1=17200:b2 = 20200: b3=25400:b4 = 33300: b5=41200

REM*** input the gross income ***
PRINT
SET #1, COLOUR (1)
 PRINT TAB(13) ; "what is your gross income";
 INPUT income

REM*** input the total allowances ***
PRINT :PRINT TAB (10); "What are your total allowances";
INPUT allow

REM*** calculate taxable amount ***
taxinc = income-allow
PRINT:PRINT TAB(15);

REM*** goto relevant procedure to calculate tax ***
IF taxinc > 0 AND taxinc <= b1 THEN GOTO tax1
IF taxinc > b1 AND taxinc <= b2 THEN GOTO tax2
IF taxinc > b2 AND taxinc <= b3 THEN GOTO tax3
IF taxinc > b3 AND taxinc <= b4 THEN GOTO tax4
IF taxinc > b4 AND taxinc <= b5 THEN GOTO tax5
IF taxinc >b5 THEN GOTO tax6

LABEL tax1
tax = taxinc * 0.29
PRINT "Tax due = £";tax :GOTO finite

LABEL tax2
tax= b1*0.29+(taxinc-b1)*0.4
PRINT "Tax due = £";tax :GOTO finite

LABEL tax3
tax = b1*0.29+(b2-b1)*0.4+(taxinc-b2)*0.45
PRINT "Tax due = £";tax :GOTO finite
```

```
LABEL tax4
tax = b1*0.29+(b2-b1)*0.4+(b3-b2)*0.45
tax = tax +(taxinc-b3)*0.5
PRINT "Tax due = £";tax :GOTO finite

LABEL tax5
tax =4988+1200+2340+3950
tax = tax+ (taxinc -b4)*0.55
PRINT "Tax due = £";tax :GOTO finite

LABEL tax6
tax = 16823+(taxinc-b5)*0.6
PRINT "Tax due = £";tax :GOTO finite

REM*** loop to stop screen being corrupted ***

LABEL finite
GOTO finite
```

Unit Conversions

```
File  Program  Edit  Fonts  Colours  Patterns  Lines  Windows     BASIC2
┌──┬──────────────────────────────────────────────────────┐
│ M│                  UNIT CONVERSIONS                      │
├──┴──────────────────────────────────────────────────────┤
│                                                          │
│      To Convert:                                         │
│                                                          │
│      1: Gallons to Litres                                │
│      2: Litres to Gallons                                │
│      3: Pounds to Kilograms                              │
│      4: Kilograms to pounds                              │
│      5: Feet and inches to Metres                        │
│      6: Metres to Feet and inches                        │
│      7: Degrees C to Degrees F                           │
│      8: Degrees F to Degrees C                           │
│                                                          │
│      enter number of gallons ?4                          │
│                                                          │
│      4 Gallons = 18.184 Litres                           │
│                                                          │
│      Press any key for another conversion, [ENTER] to stop.│
│                                                          │
└──────────────────────────────────────────────────────────┘
```

This is a program involving simple arithmetic, but which has been "dressed up" to make it more appealing to use.

The text all appears on a graphics screen, and so the font features can be fully exploited, for instance large text and bold text. The user simply has to press the number key relating to the conversion required, and then enters the number of units to convert. The equivalent value of units is then displayed.

The drop shadow effect on the headline "To Convert:" was achieved by MOVEing to the desired text position and printing the text in black, then MOVEing slightly up and to the left of the desired position and printing the text in yellow with a MODE of 2. MODE 2 is the transparent mode, so only the text and not it's white rectangular background is printed.

The ON n GOSUB statement tells the program to GOSUB to the label n places along the list. So if n is 3, the program will GOSUB to the routine poundskilos. You can also use the ON ... GOTO command in Basic2.

```
REM*** initialise and title screen ***
 SCREEN #1 GRAPHICS 600 FIXED, 200 FIXED
WINDOW #1 FULL ON
WINDOW #1 TITLE "UNIT CONVERSIONS"

REM*** display options ***
SET #1, FONT 1 POINTS 15 EFFECTS 5
MOVE #1, 1000;4000
PRINT #1,  POINTS (30) "To Convert:  "
MOVE #1, 980;4030
PRINT #1, POINTS(30)  COLOUR (6) MODE (2) "To Convert:  "
PRINT:PRINT  "         1:"; EFFECTS (0);" Gallons to Litres"
PRINT "         2:"; EFFECTS(0); " Litres to Gallons"
PRINT "         3:"; EFFECTS (0);" Pounds to Kilograms "
PRINT "         4:"; EFFECTS (0);" Kilograms to pounds "
PRINT "         5:"; EFFECTS (0);" Feet and inches to Metres"
PRINT "         6:"; EFFECTS (0);" Metres to Feet and inches"
PRINT "         7:"; EFFECTS (0);" Degrees C to Degrees F  "
PRINT "         8:"; EFFECTS (0);" Degrees F to Degrees C  "
PRINT
SET #1, COLOUR(2)

REM*** input choice and safety check ***

LABEL inputloop
MOVE #1, 1000;1525
PRINT #1, "please enter your choice ";

GOSUB waitkey:REM*** wait for a key to be pressed ***

IF n$>"0" AND n$<"9" THEN GOTO calculate
MOVE #1, 000;1525
GOTO inputloop
```

■ SECTION 23
Practical

```
LABEL calculate
n = VAL(n$)

REM*** gosub to the appropriate routine ***
ON n GOSUB gallonslitres,litresgallons,poundskilos,kilospounds,feetmetres,
  metresfeet,degcdegf,degfdegc



LABEL gallonslitres
GOSUB inputvalue
INPUT #1 "gallons ";x
PRINT:PRINT #1,"          "; COLOUR (2) ;x;" Gallons = "; COLOUR (12) ; x*4.546
  ;" Litres"
GOTO moreconvert

LABEL litresgallons
GOSUB inputvalue
INPUT #1 "litres ";x
PRINT:PRINT #1,"          "; COLOUR (2) ;x;" Litres = "; COLOUR (12) ; x*0.21998
  ;" Gallons"
GOTO moreconvert

LABEL poundskilos
GOSUB inputvalue
INPUT #1 "pounds ";x
PRINT:PRINT #1,"          "; COLOUR (2) ;x;" Pounds = "; COLOUR (12) ; x*0.4536
  ;" Kilos"
GOTO moreconvert

LABEL kilospounds
GOSUB inputvalue
INPUT #1 "kilos ";x
PRINT:PRINT #1,"          "; COLOUR (2) ;x;" Kilos = "; COLOUR (12) ; x*2.2046
  ;" Litres"
GOTO moreconvert
```

Practical

```
LABEL feetmetres
GOSUB inputvalue
INPUT #1 "feet ";f
GOSUB inputvalue
INPUT #1 "inches ";i
PRINT:PRINT #1,"          "; COLOUR (2) ;f;" Feet ";i;"Inches =" COLOUR (12)
  ; (f+i/12)*0.3048 ;" metres"
GOTO moreconvert

LABEL metresfeet
GOSUB inputvalue
INPUT #1 "metres ";x
PRINT:PRINT #1,"          "; COLOUR (2) ;x;" Metres = "; COLOUR (12) ; x*3.208
  ;" Feet"; COLOUR (2);" = ";COLOUR(12); INT(x*3.208);" Feet ";(x*3.2808-INT
  (x*3.2808))*12; " Inches"
GOTO moreconvert

LABEL degcdegf
GOSUB inputvalue
INPUT #1 "degrees C ";x
PRINT:PRINT #1,"          "; COLOUR (2) ;x;" Degrees C = "; COLOUR (12) ;
  x*9/5+32 ;" Degrees F"
GOTO moreconvert

LABEL degfdegc
GOSUB inputvalue
INPUT #1 "degrees F ";x
PRINT:PRINT #1,"          "; COLOUR (2) ;x;" Degrees F = "; COLOUR (12) ;
(x-32)*5/9 ;" Degrees C"
GOTO moreconvert

REM*** ask if any more more conversions are needed ***

LABEL moreconvert
PRINT:PRINT COLOUR(15) "          Press any key for another conversion, [ENTER]
  to stop. "
MOVE #1, 100;1525
GOSUB waitkey
```

```
IF n$= CHR$(13) THEN STOP
TEXT CLEAR EOS
GOTO inputloop
REM*** routine to print common "enter number of" part of input message ***

LABEL inputvalue
MOVE #1,3200;1525
PRINT #1,"                        "
MOVE #1, 1000;1525
PRINT #1, COLOUR(2);"enter number of ";
RETURN

LABEL waitkey
n$=INKEY$
IF n$="" THEN GOTO waitkey
RETURN
```

Spreadsheet

```
File  Program  Edit  Fonts  Colours  Patterns  Lines  Windows      BASIC2
┌──────────────────────────────────────────────────────────────────────┐
│ ⊮ │          Step-by-Step SpreadSheet      Version 0.5                │
│ ◀ B1  :'TO OBTAIN CONTROL MENU TYPE /                                 │
│ ┌────────────────────────────────────────────────────────────────┐   │
│ │ ⫴ A ⫴  B ⫴  C  ⫴  D  ⫴  E ⫴  F ⫴  G  ⫴  H ⫴ I ⫴ J ⫴           │
│ 01 │     TO OBTAIN CONTROL MENU TYPE /              VERSION 0.5   │   │
│ 02 │                                                             │   │
│ 03 │     CURSOR CONTROLS ARE E/UP S/LEFT D/RIGHT AND X/DOWN       │   │
│ 04 │                                                             │   │
│ 05 │     TEXT CAN CONTINUE OVER CELLS, BUT BE CAREFUL OF THE EDGE │   │
│ 06 │                                                             │   │
│ 07 │  10.00             12.00                                    │   │
│ 08 │  20.00            100.00                                    │   │
│ 09 │ -------            32.00                                    │   │
│ 10 │  30.00 <-- A07+A08 30.00                                    │   │
│ 11 │                   -------                                   │   │
│ 12 │ THE 0 IN THE CELL  174.00 <-- D07:D10                       │   │
│ 13 │ REFERENCE MUST BE                                           │   │
│ 14 │ ENTERED.          THE COLON MEANS SUM                       │   │
│ 15 │                                                             │   │
│ └────────────────────────────────────────────────────────────────┘   │
└──────────────────────────────────────────────────────────────────────┘
```

What is a Spreadsheet?

A spreadsheet is a software program that will perform financial calculations. It is simply no more than a blank sheet of paper upon which numbers and text can be entered in just the same way as one would use a sheet of paper and a pencil. The huge advantage of using a computer spreadsheet is that simple formulae can be applied to each number or series of numbers and the spreadsheet formulae will alter all the related number entries accordingly.

```
CLOSE WINDOW 1:CLOSE WINDOW 2:CLOSE WINDOW 3:CLOSE WINDOW 4
CLOSE £10:DIM spread$(10,15),values(10,15)
col=1:row=1:cl=1:rw=0:blank$="        "

SCREEN £1,TEXT 80 FIXED, 25 FIXED INFORMATION ON
WINDOW £1,PLACE 3,20
```

```
WINDOW £1 TITLE "Step-by-Step SpreadSheet    Version 0.5"
GOSUB draw_sheet:WINDOW £1 OPEN
SCREEN £2,TEXT 80 FIXED,4 FIXED INFORMATION ON
WINDOW £2,PLACE 3,4:WINDOW £2 TITLE "Step-by-Step Directory screen"
GOTO cursor_movement


LABEL scan_keys
  key_pres$=UPPER$(INKEY$):IF key_pres$="" THEN GOTO scan_keys
RETURN


LABEL cursor_movement
  GOSUB inverse_data:GOSUB get_info:WINDOW £1,INFORMATION info$
LABEL cursor_keys
  GOSUB scan_keys
  IF key_pres$="S" AND col> 1 THEN cl=-1:rw=0:GOTO norm_data
  IF key_pres$="D" AND col<10 THEN cl= 1:rw=0:GOTO norm_data
  IF key_pres$="E" AND row> 1 THEN rw=-1:cl=0:GOTO norm_data
  IF key_pres$="X" AND row<15 THEN rw= 1:cl=0:GOTO norm_data
  IF key_pres$="/" THEN GOSUB get_mode:GOTO cursor_movement
  GOTO cursor_keys
LABEL norm_data
  PRINT £1,AT(col*7-1;row+2);inverse$:col=col+cl:row=row+rw
GOTO cursor_movement


LABEL get_mode
  WINDOW £1,INFORMATION "C-Cursor F-Form '-Text £-Numbers L-Load S-Save
    D-reDraw P-Print Z-Zap Q-Quit"
LABEL get_mode_key
  GOSUB scan_keys
  IF key_pres$="C" THEN RETURN
  IF key_pres$="Z" THEN GOTO zap
  IF key_pres$="F" THEN GOTO formulae_entry
  IF key_pres$="'" THEN GOTO text_entry
  IF key_pres$="£" THEN GOTO number_entry
  IF key_pres$="L" THEN GOTO load_sheet
  IF key_pres$="S" THEN GOTO save_sheet
  IF key_pres$="D" THEN GOTO draw_sheet
  IF key_pres$="P" THEN GOTO print_sheet
```

Business

```
    IF key_pres$="Q" THEN GOTO quit_sheet
  GOTO get_mode_key

LABEL draw_sheet
  CLS £1
  WINDOW £1,INFORMATION "REDRAWING SHEET,  PLEASE WAIT"
  PRINT £1,AT(1;2);"     ";
  FOR loop=1 TO 10
    PRINT £1,EFFECTS(64);"¦ ";CHR$(loop+64);" ¦";
  NEXT loop
  FOR loop=1 TO 15
    axi$=STR$(loop):IF loop<10 THEN axi$=" 0"+axi${2}
    PRINT £1,AT(1;loop+2);axi$;TAB(5);"¦"
  NEXT loop
  FOR loop1=1 TO 15:FOR loop2=1 TO 10
    eval_col=loop2:eval_row=loop1
    GOSUB eval_cell:IF content$="" THEN GOTO empty_cell
    PRINT £1,AT(loop2*7-1;loop1+2);blank$
    PRINT £1,AT(loop2*7-1;loop1+2);content$
LABEL empty_cell
  NEXT loop2,loop1
  GOSUB inverse_data
RETURN

LABEL eval_cell
  content$=spread$(eval_col,eval_row):IF content$="" THEN RETURN
  control$=content${1}:IF control$="'" THEN content$=content${2 TO}:RETURN
  IF control$="!" THEN GOTO calc_formulae
  values(eval_col,eval_row)=VAL(content$)
  content$=DEC$(VAL(content$),"£££££££")    'Change to suit need
RETURN

LABEL inverse_data
  eval_col=col:eval_row=row:GOSUB eval_cell
  inverse$=content${TO 7}:fl$=blank$:IF inverse$="" THEN inverse$=blank$
  IF LEN(inverse$)<7 THEN fl${1 TO LEN(inverse$)}=inverse$:inverse$=fl$
  PRINT £1,EFFECTS(64);AT(col*7-1;row+2);inverse$
RETURN
```

```
LABEL calc_formulae
  content$=content${2 TO}:sum=0:cont$="":pass=0:col_temp=0:row_temp=0
  REPEAT
    col_temp_sum=col_temp:col_temp=ASC(content${1})-64
    row_temp_sum=row_temp:row_temp=VAL(content${2 TO 3})
    answer=values(col_temp,row_temp):IF pass=0 THEN sum=answer
    IF cont$="+" THEN sum=sum+answer
    IF cont$="-" THEN sum=sum-answer
    IF cont$="/" THEN sum=sum/answer
    IF cont$="*" THEN sum=sum*answer
    IF cont$=":" THEN GOSUB sum
    cont$=content${4}:content$=content${5 TO}:pass=1
  UNTIL content$=""
  values(col,row)=sum:content$=DEC$(sum,"ffffffff") 'Change to suit need
RETURN

LABEL sum
  sum_temp=0:FOR col_i=col_temp_sum TO col_temp
    FOR row_j=row_temp_sum TO row_temp
      sum_temp=sum_temp+values(col_i,row_j)
    NEXT row_j,col_i:sum=sum_temp
RETURN

LABEL get_info
  IF cl= 1 THEN info$=CHR$(14)
  IF cl=-1 THEN info$=CHR$(15)
  IF rw= 1 THEN info$=CHR$(13)
  IF rw=-1 THEN info$=CHR$(12)
  content$=spread$(col,row):IF content$="" THEN content$="BLANK"
  info$=info$+" "+STR$(row)+"  :"+content$:info${3}=CHR$(64+col)
RETURN

LABEL formulae_entry
  data$="":in$="+-/*:0123456789ABCDEFGHIJ"+CHR$(8)+CHR$(13)
  REPEAT
LABEL next_form
    WINDOW £1,INFORMATION "Formulae Entry >"+data$
    GOSUB scan_keys:IF INSTR(in$,key_pres$)=0 THEN GOTO next_form
```

SECTION 24
Business

```
    IF key_pres$<>CHR$(8) THEN GOTO add_form
    data$=data$(TO -2):GOTO next_form
LABEL add_form
    data$=data$+key_pres$
  UNTIL key_pres$=CHR$(13)
  data$=data$(TO -2):data$="!"+data$
  spread$(col,row)=data$:values(col,row)=0
  PRINT £1,AT(col*7-1;row+2);blank$:content$=data$:GOSUB calc_formulae
  PRINT £1,AT(col*7-1;row+2);content$:GOSUB next_cell:GOSUB inverse_data
RETURN

LABEL text_entry
  data$=""
  REPEAT
LABEL next_letter
    WINDOW £1,INFORMATION "Text Entry >"+data$:GOSUB scan_keys
    IF key_pres$=CHR$(8) THEN data$=data$(TO -2):GOTO next_letter
LABEL add_letter
    data$=data$+key_pres$
  UNTIL key_pres$=CHR$(13)
  data$=data$(TO -2):PRINT £1,AT(col*7-1;row+2);blank$
  PRINT £1,AT(col*7-1;row+2);data$:data$="'"+data$
  spread$(col,row)=data$:values(col,row)=0:GOSUB next_cell
  GOSUB inverse_data
RETURN

LABEL number_entry
  data$="":in$=".0123456789"+CHR$(8)+CHR$(13)
  REPEAT
    WINDOW £1,INFORMATION "Number Entry >"+data$
LABEL not_num
    GOSUB scan_keys
    IF INSTR(in$,key_pres$)=0 THEN GOTO not_num
    IF key_pres$=CHR$(8) THEN data$=data$(TO -2):GOTO next_num
    data$=data$+key_pres$
LABEL next_num
  UNTIL key_pres$=CHR$(13)
  data$=data$(TO -2):values(col,row)=VAL(data$)
```

140

```
    content$=DEC$(values(col,row),"£££££££"):spread$(col,row)=content$
    PRINT £1,AT(col*7-1;row+2);blank$:PRINT £1,AT(col*7-1;row+2);content$
    GOSUB next_cell:GOSUB inverse_data
RETURN


LABEL next_cell
  IF cl=-1 AND col>1 THEN col=col-1
  IF cl= 1 AND col<10 THEN col=col+1
  IF rw=-1 AND row>1  THEN row=row-1
  IF rw= 1 AND row<15 THEN row=row+1
RETURN


LABEL load_sheet
  WINDOW £1,INFORMATION "LOAD A NEW SPREADSHEET"
REPEAT
  CLS £2:file_no=1
  REPEAT
    file$=FIND$("*.cal",file_no):PRINT £2,file$,:file_no=file_no+1
  UNTIL file$=""
  WINDOW £2,OPEN:data$=""
  in$="ABCDEFGHIJKLMNOPQRSTUVWXYZ0123456789_"+CHR$(8)+CHR$(13)
  REPEAT
LABEL next_load
    WINDOW £2,INFORMATION "Enter filename (max 8 Chars .cal added) >"+data$
    GOSUB scan_keys:IF key_pres$=" " THEN key_pres$="_"
    IF INSTR(in$,key_pres$)=0 THEN GOTO next_load
    IF key_pres$<>CHR$(8) THEN GOTO add_load
    data$=data${TO -2}:GOTO next_load
LABEL add_load
    data$=data$+key_pres$
  UNTIL LEN(data$)=8 OR key_pres$=CHR$(13)
  IF key_pres$=CHR$(13) THEN data$=data${ TO -2}
  data$=data$+".cal"
UNTIL FIND$(data$)<>""
  OPEN £10 INPUT data$
  FOR loop1=1 TO 10:FOR loop2=1 TO 15
    INPUT £10,in$:INPUT £10,values(loop1,loop2):IF in$="@&" THEN in$=""
    spread$(loop1,loop2)=UPPER$(in$)
```

```
'    WINDOW £1,INFORMATION "Loading "+STR$(loop1)+":"+STR$(loop2)
     NEXT loop2,loop1
     INPUT £10,col:INPUT £10,row:CLOSE £10:CLS £1:CLOSE WINDOW 2
     GOSUB draw_sheet
RETURN

LABEL save_sheet
   WINDOW £1,INFORMATION "SAVE SPREADSHEET"
   CLS £2:file_no=1
   REPEAT
     file$=FIND$("*.cal",file_no)
     PRINT £2,file$,
     file_no=file_no+1
   UNTIL file$=""
   WINDOW £2,OPEN
   data$=""
   in$="ABCDEFGHIJKLMNOPQRSTUVWXYZ0123456789_"+CHR$(8)+CHR$(13)
   REPEAT
LABEL next_save
     WINDOW £2,INFORMATION "Enter filename (max 8 Chars .cal added) >"+data$
     GOSUB scan_keys:IF key_pres$=" " THEN key_pres$="_"
     IF INSTR(in$,key_pres$)=0 THEN GOTO next_save
     IF key_pres$<>CHR$(8) THEN GOTO add_save
     data$=data${TO -2):GOTO next_save
LABEL add_save
     data$=data$+key_pres$
   UNTIL LEN(data$)=8 OR key_pres$=CHR$(13)
   IF key_pres$=CHR$(13) THEN data$=data${ TO -2)
   data$=data$+".cal":OPEN £10 OUTPUT data$
   FOR loop1=1 TO 10:FOR loop2=1 TO 15:out$=spread$(loop1,loop2)
     IF out$="" THEN out$="a&"
     PRINT £10,out$:PRINT £10,values(loop1,loop2)
'      WINDOW £1,INFORMATION "Saving "+STR$(loop1)+":"+STR$(loop2)
     NEXT loop2,loop1
   PRINT £10,col:PRINT £10,row:CLOSE £10:CLOSE WINDOW 2
RETURN
```

Business

```
LABEL zap
    WINDOW £1,INFORMATION "ZAP Data  A-All R-Row C-Column SPACE-Current cell"
    GOSUB scan_keys
    IF key_pres$="A" THEN sl1= 1:sl2=1  :el1=10 :el2=15 :GOTO confirm_zap
    IF key_pres$="R" THEN sl1= 1:sl2=row:el1=10 :el2=row:GOTO confirm_zap
    IF key_pres$="C" THEN sl1=col:sl2=1  :el1=col:el2=15 :GOTO confirm_zap
    IF key_pres$=" " THEN sl1=col:sl2=row:el1=col:el2=row:GOTO confirm_zap
    RETURN
LABEL confirm_zap
    WINDOW £1,INFORMATION "Confirm ZAP cells (Y/N)":GOSUB scan_keys
    IF key_pres$<>"Y" THEN RETURN
LABEL zap_cells
    FOR loop1=sl1 TO el1:FOR loop2=sl2 TO el2
      spread$(loop1,loop2)="":values(loop1,loop2)=0
    NEXT loop2,loop1:GOSUB draw_sheet
RETURN

LABEL print_sheet
LPRINT CHR$(15);"    ";
FOR loop=1 TO 10:LPRINT"! ";CHR$(loop+64);" !";:NEXT loop:LPRINT
FOR loop1=1 TO 15:LPRINT loop1;TAB(5);"!";
    FOR loop2=1 TO 10:eval_row=loop1:eval_col=loop2:GOSUB eval_cell
    LPRINT content$;:NEXT loop2:LPRINT:NEXT loop1
RETURN

LABEL quit_sheet
    WINDOW £1,INFORMATION "QUIT SPREADSHEET (Y/N) WARNING ALL DATA WILL BE LOST"
    PRINT STRING$(2,CHR$(7)):GOSUB scan_keys
    IF key_pres$="Y" THEN CLEAR RESET:END
RETURN
```

Database

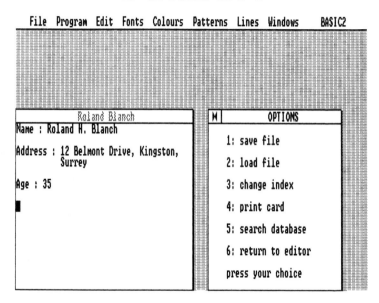

This program was written to demonstrate how to handle random files. The text editor therefore is extremely simple; you can type in text and carriage returns, or you can delete the previous character. There is no facility to move through the text, so pay close attention to what you type, as the only way of correcting anything is to delete the offending character.

To do anything with the card you are editing, you need to press the "+" key to bring up the menu.

The options are selected by pressing the appropriate key on the main keyboard, and behave as follows:

1: save file

This simply saves the card you are currently working on. It creates the filename by taking the first eight letters of the card's index (the name displayed in the title bar of the first window). A short routine then replaces any spaces in the filename with underscores("_"), as spaces will be rejected by the computer. The extension "crd" is then added, and the file saved to disk A.

2: load file

This displays all your cards' filenames by using the FILES #1,"*.crd" statement to list in window 1 all files with the crd extension.

The user is then asked which card is required. The filename only needs to be entered; the ".crd" part is added by the program. The program then defines the variable "check" as being the code returned by a test opening of the required file. If check is greater than 100 then the requested file does not exist, and the user is informed. A new required filename must then be entered, and if it exists, the file will be loaded.

3: change index

The name of the card, for instance an employee name or item description, is shown in the title bar (the one line box at the top of the first window.)

If the change index option is selected, you simply type in the new name for the index and press return. You will see it change in the title bar instantly. This is done using the TITLE command, specifically for WINDOW #1.

4: print card

This option prints out the card index followed by the information on the card. You have to check that your printer is set up correctly and on line, then press any key for the print to start.

5: search database

This option requires you to type in a line of text. The program will then search through all card files on your disk. Any file containing the inputted text will be displayed, and the option to print the file will be given.
This is useful for searching for files of all people living in a certain street, or all items with the same manufacturer etc.

6: return to editor

This option simply turns off the options window and allows you to carry on editing the current card.

```
CLOSE WINDOW 1:CLOSE WINDOW 2:CLOSE WINDOW 3:CLOSE WINDOW 4
CLOSE £3:CLOSE £4:CLOSE £5
SCREEN £1, TEXT 40 FIXED,15 FIXED:WINDOW £1, PLACE 1;1
SET £1, MODE (1):WINDOW CURSOR ON:SET WRAP ON:WINDOW £1,OPEN

text$=CHR$(13)+CHR$(13)+CHR$(13):title$=" NOT-NAMED":WINDOW £1 TITLE title$
curs=4:PRINT £1,AT(1;1);text$;

LABEL inputloop
an$=INKEY$:IF an$="" THEN GOTO inputloop
IF curs=599 THEN GOTO delcheck
IF an$="+" THEN GOTO filess
IF an$=CHR$(13) THEN curs=curs+1:PRINT CHR$(10);:text$=text$+CHR$(10)
text$=text$+an$:PRINT £1,MODE(2);text${curs};
IF text${curs-1)=CHR$(13) THEN crfl =1 ELSE crfl =0

LABEL delcheck
IF NOT(an$=CHR$(8)) THEN GOTO con
IF curs<5 THEN GOTO con
al=(LEN(text$)+1)-curs-crfl:b$=LEFT$(text$,curs-2)+RIGHT$(text$,al)
curs=curs-2-crfl:bl=(LEN(b$)-1):text$=LEFT$(b$,bl)

IF curs > 5 AND crfl = 1 THEN CLS:PRINT £1,AT(1;1);text$;:GOTO con
PRINT " "; CHR$(8);

LABEL con
IF curs>=599 THEN GOTO inputloop
curs=curs+1:GOTO inputloop

LABEL filess
CLOSE £4:CLOSE WINDOW 4:OPEN £4,WINDOW 4:SCREEN £4 TEXT 30 FIXED, 15 FIXED
WINDOW £4 PLACE 350;1:WINDOW £4 TITLE "OPTIONS":WINDOW £4 OPEN
```

■ SECTION 24
Business

```
LABEL options
WINDOW £4,OPEN:CLS £4
PRINT £4,,"   1: save file"      :PRINT £4,,"   2: load file"
PRINT £4,,"   3: change index"   :PRINT £4,,"   4: print card"
PRINT £4,,"   5: search database" :PRINT £4,,"   6: return to editor"
PRINT £4,,"   press your choice"

LABEL choiceloop
c$=INKEY$:IF c$<"1" OR c$>"6" THEN GOTO choiceloop
c=VAL(c$):ON c GOSUB savefile,loadfile,indexchange,printfile,searchbase
CLS £4:IF c=6 THEN WINDOW £4 CLOSE:CLOSE £4:GOTO inputloop
GOTO options

LABEL savefile
CLS £4:CLOSE £5:h$=title$:file$=LEFT$(title$,8)+".crd"
FOR nl=1 TO 8:IF file${nl}=" " THEN file${nl}="_"
NEXT nl
OPEN £5 RANDOM file$ LENGTH 600:PUT £5,h$:POSITION £5,NEXT:PUT £5,text$
CLOSE £5:RETURN

LABEL loadfile
IF FIND$("*.crd")<>"" THEN GOTO chloop
CLS £4:PRINT £4,"NO FILES EXIST!!";CHR$(7);CHR$(7)
FOR loop=1 TO 2000:NEXT loop:RETURN

LABEL chloop
CLS £1:FILES £1,"*.crd":PRINT £1:INPUT £1,"Which file (.crd added) ";file$
check=OPEN £5,OLD RANDOM file$+".crd":CLOSE £5
IF check>100 THEN PRINT £1,"That file does not exist":GOTO chloop
OPEN £5,RANDOM file$+".crd" LENGTH 600:GET £5,title$:POSITION £5,NEXT
GET £5,text$:CLOSE £5
WINDOW £1 TITLE title$:CLS £1:PRINT £1,text$;:curs=LEN(text$)+1:CLOSE £4
GOTO inputloop

LABEL indexchange
CLS £4:INPUT £4," New name for index";title$:WINDOW £1,TITLE title$:RETURN

LABEL printfile
CLS £4:PRINT £4,"Check your printer.":PRINT £4,"Press a key when ready."
```

```
LABEL printwait
IF INKEY$="" THEN GOTO printwait
LPRINT CHR$(27);"W";CHR$(1):LPRINT title$
LPRINT CHR$(27);"W";CHR$(0)+CHR$(27);"E":LPRINT text$:CLS £1:RETURN

LABEL searchbase
CLS £4:WINDOW £4,OPEN:PRINT £4,"Input text to search for:":INPUT £4,search$
IF search$="" THEN GOTO searchbase
file_no=1

IF FIND$("*.crd")="" THEN PRINT £4,"No files on disk":GOTO options

REPEAT
 file$=FIND$("*.crd",file_no):IF file$="" THEN GOTO end_search
 file_no=file_no+1:OPEN £5,RANDOM file$ LENGTH 600
 GET £5,t$:POSITION £5,NEXT:GET £5,a$
 IF INSTR(a$,search$)<>0 THEN GOSUB out_file
 CLOSE £5
UNTIL FALSE

LABEL end_search
PRINT £1,"Sorry no more files contain ";search$
FOR loop=1 TO 5000:NEXT loop
WINDOW £1,TITLE title$:CLS £1:PRINT £1,AT(1;1);text$:GOTO options

LABEL out_file
CLS £1:WINDOW £1,TITLE t$:PRINT £1,AT(1;1);a$
CLS £4:PRINT £4"Do you want this printed Y/N"
REPEAT:in$=INKEY$:UNTIL INSTR("yYnN",in$)<>0
IF INSTR("Nn",in$)<>0 THEN RETURN
LPRINT CHR$(27);"W";CHR$(1):LPRINT tt$
LPRINT CHR$(27);"W";CHR$(0)+CHR$(27);"E":LPRINT a$
RETURN
```

Wordprocessor

File Program Edit Fonts Colours Patterns Lines Windows   BASIC2

| H | | wordpro.DOC |

What is a word processor?

the computer with a word-processing package allows even the most casual typist to produce well presented, error-free documents, quickly and easily.
 The two-fingered typist can arrange the format of the page, correct any mistakes and produce material worthy of the most experienced secretary.
 The following program gives an idea of how a word processing package works. The program is limited in it's facilities in comparison to an established package such as WordStar 1512, but shows how a word processing package deals with text._

```
REM*** press Esc to get menu up ***
REM*** save files with '.DOC', this will avoid confusion ***

CLEAR RESET
CLOSE WINDOW 1:CLOSE WINDOW 2
CLOSE WINDOW 3:CLOSE WINDOW 4
SCREEN #1,TEXT 80 FIXED,20 FIXED
WINDOW #1,CURSOR OFF:WINDOW #1,PLACE 3;4
CLOSE #5

DIM lines(100),text$(20) FIXED 70
lines(0) = 1

LABEL start_prog
FOR i=1 TO 20
text$(i)=STRING$(79,32)
NEXT i
```

```
SCREEN #2,TEXT 80 FIXED,10 FIXED INFORMATION ON
WINDOW #2,PLACE 3;135:

LABEL main_menu
CLS #2
WINDOW #2 TITLE "Step-by-Step Wordprocessor    Version 0.1    Opening Menu"

PRINT #2,""
PRINT #2," P  PRINT a file"
PRINT #2,""
PRINT #2," D  Open a file"
PRINT #2,""
PRINT #2," S  save file "
IF file$<>"" THEN PRINT #2:print#2," R Return to current Document"

WINDOW #2 OPEN

LABEL read_a_key
key_pres$=INKEY$
IF key_pres$="" THEN GOTO read_a_key
IF key_pres$="d" OR key_pres$="D" THEN GOTO open_document
IF key_pres$="p" OR key_pres$="P" THEN GOTO print_file
IF key_pres$ ="s" AND file$<>"" THEN GOTO put_file
IF file$<>"" AND key_pres$="r" THEN CLOSE WINDOW 2:CLS #2:  WINDOW #1 OPEN: GO
   TO curs
GOTO read_a_key

LABEL print_file
CLS #2
FILES #2,"*.*"
INPUT #2,"Input file to print ";file$
GOSUB get_file
FOR i = 1 TO 20
LPRINT text$(i)
NEXT i
GOTO main_menu
```

```
LABEL get_file
CLS #2
CLOSE WINDOW 2
OPEN #5,INPUT file$
FOR i = 1 TO 20
INPUT #5,text$(i)
INPUT #5,lines(i)
NEXT i
INPUT #5,col
INPUT #5,row
CLOSE #5
IF key_pres$="d" THEN GOTO draw_words
RETURN

LABEL put_file
OPEN #5, OUTPUT file$
FOR i = 1 TO 20
PRINT #5, text$(i)
PRINT #5, lines(i)
NEXT i
PRINT #5,col
PRINT #5,row
CLOSE #5
WINDOW #2 INFORMATION "Document saved as "+file$
GOTO read_a_key

LABEL open_document
CLS #2:WINDOW #2,OPEN
FILES #2,"*.*"
PRINT #2,"Input name of file to edit "
INPUT #2,file$

CLOSE WINDOW 2
col = 1:row=1
WINDOW #1 TITLE UPPER$(file$):IF FIND$(file$)<>"" THEN GOSUB get_file
WINDOW #1 OPEN
```

```
LABEL draw_words
CLS #1
WINDOW #1 OPEN
FOR n = 1 TO row
PRINT #1, text$(n)
NEXT n

LABEL curs
PRINT #1,AT(col;row);"_"

key_pres$=INKEY$
PRINT #1,AT(col;row);"-"
IF key_pres$="" THEN GOTO curs
WINDOW #1 TITLE file$+" Row "+STR$(row)+"  Column" + STR$(col)


IF key_pres$=CHR$(27) THEN GOTO main_menu

LABEL ret_char
IF key_pres$<>CHR$(13) THEN GOTO del_char
PRINT #1,AT(col;row);" "
lines(row)=col
row=row+1:col=1:IF row>18 THEN row=18:col=lines(18)
GOTO curs

LABEL del_char
IF key_pres$<>CHR$(8) THEN GOTO add_letter
IF row=1 AND col=1 THEN PRINT CHR$(7):GOTO curs
PRINT #1,AT(col;row);" "
col=col-1:IF col=0 AND row>1 THEN col=lines(row-1):row=row-1
IF row=0 THEN row=1
text$(row) {col)=" "
GOTO curs

LABEL add_letter
text$(row) {col)=key_pres$
PRINT #1,AT(col;row);key_pres$
```

```
col=col+1
IF col<79 THEN GOTO curs
lines(row)=col:col=1
row=row+1:IF row>18 THEN row=18:col=lines(18)
GOTO curs
```

PART THREE

Summary of BASIC 2 Keywords

Program structure

CONT Continue a program after a CTRL-C break, or STOP.

DEF FNname(variable(s)) = **formula** Define a new function for use later in the program.

    eg. **DEF FNcube(n)** = **n * n * n**

After this line has been executed, the statement **FNcube(3)**, for example, would produce the value 27.

END marks an end to the program – there may be more than one end.

ERR gives the number of the error that has occurred.

ERROR$(number) gives the error message associated with an error number. See Section 20.

FOR var-name = **start TO end STEP size ... NEXT var-name** repeats the set of commands enclosed in the loop. The value of **var-name** is altered by **size** at the NEXT line, until **end** is reached or overshot. If omitted,the **STEP size** is taken as +1. See Section 6.

GOSUB label-name jumps to a subroutine, and returns to the jump-point afterwards. See Section 9.

GOTO label-name jumps to the named line. See Section 6.

IF condition(s) THEN command(s)-1 ELSE command(s)-2 FI. Only the first half of this line is essential, and **command(s)-1** will be performed if the condition(s) are met. Where **ELSE** is used, the commands after it will be performed if the conditions are not met. **FI** is only needed where the commands are spread over two or more lines. See Section 7.

LABEL name marks a point in the program for use with **GOTO** or **GOSUB** jumps. See Section 6.

NEW erases the current program and its variables from memory.

ON ERROR GOTO name. Redirects the program to a named error-handling routine. **ON ERROR GOTO 0** restores normal service. See Section 20

Program structure

ON var.name GOTO list.of.label.names
ON var.name GOSUB list.of.label.names. The value of **var.name** must round to between 1 and the number of label-names in the list. If the value is *n*, then the program will jump to the *nth* label-name. eg. Given the line:

ON choice GOTO draw.line,make.circle,make.box,save.pic
if **choice** has the value 3, the program will jump to **make.box**

OPTION RUN will protect a Basic program or routine by disabling Break and STOP. See Section 20.

OPTION STOP will re-enable Break and STOP.

QUIT or **SYSTEM** — exit Basic.

REM prefaces a remark. Any Basic commands further on the line will be ignored.

REPEAT .... UNTIL condition. The commands enclosed by these keywords will be repeated until the condition is met. See Section 6.

RESUME label-name will re-start the program after an error-handling routine, at the point marked by **label-name**. If this is omitted, the program will return to the command at which the error occurred. If **RESUME NEXT** is used, the program re-starts at the next command.

RETURN jumps back from a subroutine to the command after **GOSUB**. See Section 9.

RUN starts a program from the beginning, and erases all variables. Alternatively **GOTO label-name** will start execution from the named routine.

STOP can be written into a program, as an alternative to **END**, or typed in the Dialogue window (or clicked from the Program menu) to break into a program while it is running.

WHILE condition .... WEND the commands between the keywords are repeated if the condition is true, and while it remains so. See Section 6.

■ SECTION 26
Inputs and outputs

Almost all of this set of commands assume that inputs will be from the keyboard, and outputs to the default screen - *Results-1* - unless another stream is specified. # **stream-number** should be included in the line, immediately after the command word, if it is necessary.

CLS CLear the Screen and reset the cursor to the top left.

EXTENT print-items tells you the distance that would be covered by the *print-items* if PRINTed.

INKEY returns the ASCII code of the key which is pressed, or -1 if no key is down. It is normally used in a loop, to wait for a keypress.
PRINT "Press any key"
REPEAT
ky = INKEY
UNTIL ky <> -1

INKEY$ This function is almost identical to **INKEY**, but here the result is the character read from the keyboard.
PRINT "Press G to go on"
ky$ = INKEY$
UNTIL UPPER$(ky$) = "G"

INPUT AT (col;row); "prompt";variable(s) reads data from the keyboard or a disk file into a string or number variable. Only INPUT variable is essential. This assumes that the INPUT comes from the keyboard, and will be printed at the current cursor position.

INPUT$(number) is a cross between **INPUT** and **INKEY$**. It reads a given number of characters from the keyboard, but does not print them on screen. The most obvious use is for password protection.
try = 0
pass$ = INPUT$(5)
WHILE pass$ <> "OPEN!" AND try < 3
try = try + 1
pass$ = INPUT$(5)
WEND
IF try = 4 THEN PRINT "Invader!"
....

LINE INPUT .... is identical to **INPUT** except that anything that is typed on the line will be taken into the variable. The simpler form will not allow the use of commas, unless the whole string is enclosed in quotes.

LPRINT items is similar to PRINT, with output to the printer. The number of options that will work depends upon the type of printer.

LOCATE col;line moves the cursor to the given column and line. As both print and INPUT have the AT (col,line) option, this command has limited value.

MOVE x;y will move the cursor to the point on the graphics screen set by the x,y values.

POS tells you the current column of the text cursor.

PRINT items. The *items* may be printable material - text, numbers or the contents of variables — or control options which affect the position or nature of the screen display. There is no set limit to the number of items that may be given, though all must be separated by either a comma or a semi-colon. The print options are:
    AT (column;row)
    TAB(column)
    ADJUST(points-size)
    ANGLE(degrees)
    COLOUR(number 0 - 15)
    EFFECTS(bit-expression)
    FONT(number 1 - 4)
    MARGIN(column)
    MODE (number 0 - 3)
    POINTS(size 7 - 72)
    ZONE(width)
See Section 13.

SET options define the nature of the text as it appears on screen, and are the same as those given under **PRINT**. An additional option **SET WRAP ON/OFF** may also be used to control the way that text is printed when a word threatens to go off the edge of the screen.

STREAM #**number** sets the current default stream.

■ SECTION 26
Inputs and outputs

TEXT options give you control over a text screen. Whatever the option, the operaton will begin from the current cursor position.
  TEXT DELETE - erase a character
  TEXT DELETE LINE - move text down to insert a line
  TEXT FEED number - move the cursor up or down a number of lines
  TEXT CLEAR EOL - delete from cursor to End Of Line
  TEXT CLEAR BOL - delete from Beginning Of Line to cursor
  TEXT CLEAR EOS - delete from cursor to End Of Screen
  TEXT CLEAR BOS - delete from Beginning Of Screen to cursor
  TEXT CLEAR SCREEN - equivalent to a simple **CLS**

TYPE see **DISPLAY**

VPOS returns the line number of the cursor.

XPOS returns the x co-ordinate of the cursor.

XPOS returns the y co-ordinate of the cursor.

■ SECTION 27
Windows and screens

SCREEN #stream **GRAPHICS** options
SCREEN #stream **TEXT** options
SCREEN #stream **TEXT FLEXIBLE** options
Define a virtual screen for use with either graphics or text. The options are:
width FIXED, height FIXED sets the size of the screen. If **FIXED** is used, the window's dimensions must be the same as the screen.
MAXIMUM width,height sets a maximum size for the window.
MINIMUM width,height sets a minimum size for the window.
UNIT width-step, height-step sets minimum amounts by which the size of the window may change.
INFORMATION ON/OFF turns the information line on and off. See Section 10.

WINDOW CLOSE removes a window from the display.
WINDOW CURSOR ON/OFF shows or hides the cursor.
WINDOW FULL ON/OFF switches between full and current size.
WINDOW INFORMATION string gives the text to be written on the line
WINDOW OPEN brings a window into the display.
WINDOW PLACE x;y moves the window to the place given by the x;y co-ordinates of its bottom left corner.
WINDOW SCROLL x;y moves the window over its virtual screen.
WINDOW SIZE width,height sets the window to a new size.
WINDOW TITLE string gives the text to be written on the title line

XPLACE and **YPLACE** give the co-ordinates of a window.
XVIRTUAL and **YVIRTUAL** give the current sizes of a screen.
XWINDOW and **YWINDOW** give the current sizes of a window.

■ SECTION 28
Graphics

All graphics drawing commands can include options to set the style and nature of the graphic display. See Sections 3, 4 and 11.

ARC start-x;start-y , end-x;end-y , radius options. You must give the x;y co-ordinates of the start and end of the arc — noting that the line will be drawn anti-clockwise. The options are **COLOUR, MODE, STYLE, WIDTH, START,** and **END**

BOX x;y , width , height options. See Sections 3 and 11.

CIRCLE x;y , radius options. See Sections 3 and 11.

ELLIPSE x;y , radius , ratio options. This produces a distorted circle, where the x radius is given by **radius**, and the y radius is the x value times the **ratio**. So **ELLIPSE 2000;2000,100,0.5** would draw an ellipse that was half as high as it was wide. The options are the same as for **CIRCLE**.

ELLIPTICAL ARC x;y , radius , ratio options is identical to **ARC** except that the arc can be distorted by the **ratio**. Likewise, **ELLIPTICAL PIE** ... is a variation on **PIE**.

FLOOD x;y boundary-colour options will start from the x;y co-ordinates and fill an area with colour, until it reaches boundaries of the given colour. The options are **COLOUR, MODE, FILL WITH.** (Does not work with certain versions of Desktop.)

GRAPHICS options resets the default values for the options.

LINE x1;y1 , x2;y2 ,... options. See Section 11.

MOVE x;y moves the graphics cursor without drawing.

PLOT x1;y1 , x2;y2 , ... options See Section 11.

SHAPE x1;y1 , x2;y2 , .. options See Section 11.

TEST x;y returns the colour of a given point.

USER ORIGIN x;y moves the origin (point 0,0) of the x;y co-ordinate system from the bottom left to the given point.

Graphics

USER SPACE width,height allows you to define your own co-ordinate system. See Section 11.

The mouse and the turtle

BUTTON (number) This checks the given mouse button to see if it is pressed, perhaps in combination with other keys. See Section 112.

DISTANCE (x;y) gives the distance of a point from the turtle.

FD or **FORWARD number-of-points options** moves the turtle forward on its current heading, drawing a line. See Section 15. The style of the line can be set by the options:

COLOUR number 0 to 15
MODE number 0 to 3
STYLE number 1 to 6
WIDTH number 1,3,5 or 7 } - see Lines menu
START number 0 to 2
END number 0 to 2

GRAPHICS CURSOR 3 selects the turtle cursor

HEADING gives the current bearing of the turtle, if in use.

LT or **LEFT(angle)** will turn the turtle through a given angle to the left.

MOVE FORWARD distance moves the turtle without drawing.

POINT angle will turn the turtle to point in the direction given in degrees.

RT or **RIGHT(angle)** will turn the turtle through a given angle to the right.

TOWARD (x;y) gives the bearing of a point from the current turtle position.

WINDOW CURSOR ON/OFF makes the turtle appear/disappear.

XMOUSE gives the x co-ordinate of the mouse pointer in pixels.

YMOUSE gives the y co-ordinate of the mouse pointer in pixels.

■ SECTION 30
String handling

ASC(string) gives the ASCII code of the first character in the string.

BIN$(number) converts a number into its binary form as a string.
BIN$(85) gives **"01010101"**.

CHR$(code) convert an ASCII code into a character.

DEC$(number,template) converts a number into a string, with the representation set by the *template*. The templates are the same here as in the **PRINT USING** command.

HEX$(number) converts a number into its hexadecimal form as a string.
HEX$(128) gives "&80".

INSTR(start-point,string,string-to-look-for) See Section 18.

LEFT$(string,number) slices a number of characters off the left-hand side of a string.
LEFT$("Locomotive Basic 2",4) gives **"Loco"**.

LEN(string) returns the number of characters in a given string.

LOWER$(string) converts a string into lower case.

MID$(string,start,length) See Section 18.

RIGHT$(string,number) slices a number of characters off the right-hand side of a string.
RIGHT$("Amstrad PC",2) gives **"PC"**.

STR$(number) converts a number into its string form, perhaps to transfer it to a string variable.
eg. **a$ = STR$(123)** gives **"123"** to the variable a$.
This may be useful in some checking and display routines.

STRING$(length,character). See Section 18.

UPPER$(string) converts a string into upper case.

WHOLE$(string). If the text stored in a fixed length string variable is not long enough, the remaining spaces are filled with *nulls* (CHR$(0)). Normally these are ignored when the variable is later used. WHOLE$ returns the entire contents of the variable, including any nulls.

■ SECTION 31
Mathematical commands and functions

ABS(number) This function returns the absolute value of a number, ignoring the sign. **ABS(-99) = ABS (99) = 99**. Its main use is for checking the difference between two values — no matter which is larger.

IF ABS(result - answer) < .1 THEN PRINT "Near enough!"

ACOS(cosine value) Give a Cosine to this function and it will return the angle. eg. If you are working in degrees then **COS(60) = 0.5**, and **ACOS(0.5) = 60**

AND Logical operator. See Section 7.

ASIN(value) Similar to ACOS, this converts Sines to Angles.

ATAN(value) or **ATN(value)** Is similar to ACOS, returning the angle of a given tangent. It should not be confused with ...

ATAN2(x,y) This is more of a graphics function than a mathematical one. Given the x,y co-ordinates of a point, this will return the bearing of that point from the origin.

CEILING(number) This function rounds up any number to the next highest whole number. so **CEILING(41.3)** is **42**, and **CEILING(-7.4)** is **-7**.

CINT(number) Another means of rounding numbers, this function converts to the nearest whole number, rather than always rounding up.

COS(angle) Returns the COSine of an angle. This may be given in either Radians or Degrees, depending upon the mode in use.

DEG(value in radians) This function converts radians into degrees. It is the same as multiplying by 360/(PI * 2) –and quicker to type.

EXP(number) is equivalent to *e* to the power of **num**. It returns the exponential of a number, and is the inverse of the LOG function.

FIX or **INT(number)**. Is the opposite of **CEILING**. It always rounds down to the nearest whole number

■ SECTION 31

Mathematical commands and functions

FRAC(number) could be seen as the opposite of **FIX**. It returns the decimal part of a number, ignoring the integer part.

LOG(number) Returns the natural logarithm (to the base e of a number).

LOG10(number) Gives a number's logarithm in base 10.

MAX(list of items) Picks the largest value out of a list. If a = 5, b = 10, c = 3 and d = 8, then **MAX(a,b,c,d)** would return the value 10.

MIN(list) Similar to **MAX**, this finds the smallest value in a list.

MOD This is used as an operator in integer arithmetic to find the remainder when a number is divided by another. **19 MOD 4** would return the value **3**. To find how many times a number will divide into another, use the backslash sign. **27 \6** gives **4**, though the operation **27 / 6** would give **3.5**.

NOT Logical operator. See Section 7.

OPTION DEGREES sets the computer to perform all angle calculations in degrees. Similarly

OPTION RADIANS specifies the use of radians. See Section 17.

OR Logical Operator. See Section 7.

PI can be used in the same way as a variable, except that its value (3.141...) is set by Basic 2 and may not be changed.

RAD(value in degrees) converts angles in degrees to their equivalent in radians.

RANDOMISE number allows you to set the start-point of the random number sequence. If **number** is omitted the command will fix the start of the sequence to a value based on **TIME**. See Section 17.

RND(number) produces a pseudo-random number in the range 0 to **number**. See Section 17.

■ SECTION 31

Mathematical commands and functions

ROUND(number,decimal places) allows you to round a number to a set number of decimal places. Thus **ROUND(12.2345,2)** gives **12.35**.

SGN(number) tells you if a number is positive, zero or negative. The value returned will be -1, 0 or 1.

    sign = SGN(num)
    IF sign = -1 THEN PRINT "negative number."
    IF sign = 1 THEN PRINT "positive number."
    IF sign = 0 THEN PRINT "The value of num is 0."

SIN(angle) gives the sine of an angle.

SQR(number) gives the square root of a number — this must be a positive value.

TAN(angle) gives the tangent of an angle.

VAL(string) finds the value of a number in a string. The evaluation stops at the first inappropriate character. It will evaluate numbers in binary or hexadecimal form, as well as normal decimals. Binary strings must start with **&X**, and hexadecimals must start with **&**.

    e.g. **VAL("123abc567")** gives a value of **123**;
    while **VAL("&X10100011")** gives **163**
    and **VAL("&BA")** gives **186**.

XOR Logical operator. See Section 7.

Data and variables

CLEAR erases all variables from memory.

DATA marks the beginning of a list of data items. See Section 16.

DIM name(dimensions) type creates an array of the given name and dimensions. See Section 16.

DIMENSIONS name gives the number of dimensions—though not their sizes — in the named array.

FRE tells you the amount of free memory space in bytes.

LET variable = **expression** assigns the value of the expression to the stated variable. The **expression** can be any combination of variables, functions and literal data that is suitable for the type of variable. **LET** is optional. The assignment will work without it.

LOWER(name,number) checks the named array and gives the lower limit of the numbered dimension.

LSET variable$ = **string**. This is only used where you want to give a value to a string variable without changing the current length of that variable. The new string will be chopped to fit, if too long, or padded with extra spaces at the end if too short. The command is useful for keeping screen displays tidy.

The length of the variable may have been **FIXED** in a RECORD or array definition; or may have been set by a previous assignment.
eg. **LET a$** = **"template 19 letters"**
LSET a$ = **"this very long string of characters"**

After this, **a$** will hold **"this very long stri"**

READ variable(s) assigns values to variables from DATA lines. See Section 16.

RECORD type-name;fields defines a type of record structure, and is mainly used to group data for filing on disk. While an array is used to link together variables of the same type, records can link variables of different types. These are defined in **fields** and may be any number variable, FIXED length string or one-dimensional array.

■ SECTION 32
Data and variables

RESTORE label-name moves the data pointer to the named line in the program. **RESTORE** moves the pointer to the first DATA line. See Section 16.

RSET variable$ = **string** is the same as **LSET** except that any cutting or padding will take place at the start of the string.

SWAP name-1,name-2 swaps the contents of the two named variables, **name-1** and **name-2**.

UPPER(name,number) checks the named array and gives the upper limit of the numbered dimension.

Time and Date

DATE(date in string) gives the number of days from 31st December 1899 to the given date. If the command is used by itself Basic 2 assumes that the current date is meant.

DATE$(number of days) converts the number into a meaningful Day, Month, Year form. It is best used in conjunction with the earlier command — **DATE$(DATE)** gives you today's date.

TIME tells you the time since midnight. The value is given in seconds. The following routine will convert this value into a more meaningful form. Note the use of integer division.

```
seconds = TIME
minutes = seconds \ 60
secs = seconds MOD 60
hours = minutes \ 60
mins = minutes MOD 60
PRINT "The time is ";hours;mins;secs
```

■ SECTION 33
Disks and sequential files

Some of the following commands may only be given directly, or at the end of a basic program line, and they will send their output to the Dialogue window. Each of these has an equivalent keyword which may be used anywhere within a Basic program, and which sends its output to any chosen stream. *Dialogue* commands are shown in italics, rather than **bold** type.

CD or **CHDIR string** changes the current directory to that given by **string**.

CHDIR$(drive-letter) tells you the name of the current directory on the given drive.

CLOSE stream number(s) Closes one or more files.See Section 19.

DEL or **KILL filename** deletes a file from a directory. See Section 19.

DIR or **FILES file-spec** show the files in a directory. If a **file-spec** is given, the command will only list those files that meet the specifications.

DISPLAY or *TYPE* **filename** will print the contents of a file.

DRIVE letter sets the drive.

EOF(#stream) tests for the End Of File, and returns a value of -1 if true. See Section 19.

FIND$(filespec,n) searches the disk for a file meeting the specifications and returns the full file-name. **n** is optional, but if given specifies that the **nth** file of that type is the one that is wanted. So, the line **name$ = FIND$("*.DAT",2)** would give to **name$** the name of the second file that has a .DAT ending.

FINDDIR$(dir-spec,n) is equivalent to **FIND$**, used to find a specified directory.

INPUT #stream,variable reads data from a file. See Section 19.

LOF(#stream) tells you the length of the current file on the given stream.

■ SECTION 33
Disks and sequential files

MD or **MKDIR string** creates a new directory, as defined in **string**.

NAME old-name AS new-name or *REN old-name new-name* renames a file.

OPEN #stream type file-name gives access to a disk file for reading or writing. The **stream** number can be from 3 to 15 (streams 0, 1 and 2 are usually reserved for the printer and screens); the **type** may be:
> **INPUT** - read a file
> **OUTPUT** - create a new file
> **NEW OUTPUT** - check that the file does not exist before attempting to create it
> **APPEND** - add to an existing file, or create one if needed
> **OLD APPEND** - check that file exists before attempting to add

RD or **RMDIR dir-spec** removes (erases) the specified directory.

RESET drive-letter resets the drive so that a new disk may be used.